THE
IRLEN
REVOLUTION

A GUIDE TO CHANGING YOUR
PERCEPTION AND YOUR LIFE

HELEN IRLEN

SQUAREONE
PUBLISHERS

COVER DESIGNER: Jeannie Tudor
EDITOR: Michele D'Altorio
TYPESETTER: Gary A. Rosenberg

The information and advice contained in this book are based upon the research and the personal and professional experiences of the author. They are not intended as a substitute for consulting with your physician or other health care provider. The publisher and author are not responsible for any adverse effects or consequences resulting from the use of any of the suggestions, preparations, or procedures discussed in this book. All matters pertaining to one's physical health should be supervised by a health care professional.

Square One Publishers
115 Herricks Road
Garden City Park, NY 11040
(516) 535-2010 • (877) 900-BOOK
www.squareonepublishers.com

Credit Line:
Images on pages 6, 7 and 8 were all found on Google Images.
Brain scans on page 101 courtesy of Amen Clinics.
Drawings on pages 134, 135, and 142 submitted by Irlen clients and printed with permission.

Library of Congress Cataloging-in-Publication Data

Irlen, Helen, 1945-
  The Irlen revolution : a guide to changing your perception and your life / Helen Irlen.
      p. cm.
  Includes bibliographical references and index.
  ISBN 978-0-7570-0236-6 (alk. paper)
  1. Perceptual disorders. 2. Learning disabilities. 3. Vision disorders. 4. Dyslexia. 5. Color vision. 6. Visual perception. I. Title.
  RC382.2.I75 2010
  362.196'85889—dc22
                                        2009052582

Printed in Canada

10   9   8   7   6   5   4   3   2   1

Contents

Acknowledgments, vi

A Note on Gender, viii

Preface, ix

Introduction, 1

1. From the Beginning, 5

2. Establishing the Irlen Method and Running
   Up Against Roadblocks, 25

3. Advocacy and Doing the Best for Your Child, 41

4. Irlen Testing: What It's All About, 57

5. Reading and Irlen Syndrome, 69

6. Irlen Syndrome Goes Beyond the Printed Page, 81

7. Light Sensitivity and Irlen Syndrome, 91

8. Headaches, Migraines, and Irlen Syndrome, 103

9. Attention Deficit Disorders and Irlen Syndrome, 117

10. Autism Spectrum Disorder and Irlen Syndrome, 129

11. Medical Conditions, Visual Conditions, and Irlen Syndrome, 145

12. Head Injuries, Psychological Problems, and Irlen Syndrome, 159

Conclusion, 173

Appendices

A. *Additional Causes of Learning Difficulties
  and Recommendations for Treatment,* 176

B. *Strategies for Dealing With Academic Problems,* 184

C. *Resources,* 193

D. *Finding an Irlen Testing Center Near You,* 203

References, 205

About the Author, 206

Index, 207

*I would like to dedicate this book to my clients
who have diligently kept journals, providing me with
knowledge of the areas of change they experienced.
To my clients who allowed me to videotape them in order
to record the changes, and to those who participated
in various research projects, providing evidence of changes.*

*You let us look inside your heads to see how your
brains function. You provided the information
that is contained in this book.*

*I feel humble in your presence and grateful for your
willingness to educate me and share your painful
stories of failures and struggles.*

Acknowledgments

It takes a family to raise a child—it is difficult to do it alone. It also takes a family to move a new idea forward. Without my "Irlen family"— clients, screeners, diagnosticians, and clinic directors—I would never have looked beyond the printed page to realize that the Irlen Method is able to help more than just those who have reading problems.

Additionally, this book would never have been possible if it were not for all of you who believed in me and in the Irlen Method. To everyone who provided guidance and support, who educated others, who risked their own jobs and professional reputations, and who put the need to help others before their own needs, thank you. The growth and expansion of Irlen is due to your support, knowledge, expertise, and experience.

As good as any method may be, it does not reach a level of acceptance without research. I am indebted to Dr. Greg Robinson, who dedicated the greater part of the last twenty years to researching the Irlen Method. He faced resistance and criticism in order to do research and publish his results, bringing the Irlen Method to a new level of acceptance and understanding within the general public and academic and research communities.

I would also like to thank Dr. Paul Whiting, Dr. Drew Yellen, Dr. Jeff Lewine, Dr. Robert Dobrin, Dr. Dan Amen, and Jim Irvine for their persistence in conducting research that has brought credibility to Irlen.

To all of you who helped spread the word about Irlen: You talked to family members, neighbors, friends, educators, and professionals; you wrote letters, articles, posted blogs, and contacted politicians; and you conducted poster sessions, presentations, and research. You chose to spread the word about Irlen. You faced opposition and challenges, but never wavered in your commitment. In doing so, you have helped make this book possible. For this, I thank you.

It has been over twenty-five years since I first discovered this amazing method. With all of you by my side, we have educated the skeptics and spread the word. Because of all that you have done and all that you continue to do, we have a voice. Together, we will make the Irlen Method available to every individual who needs this help, everywhere.

To the two people who made this book a reality: Rudy Shur and Richard Mintzer. Thank you. To my publisher, Rudy Shur, who initiated, supported, and published my first book and has continued his support by publishing this book, my heartfelt thanks. There are many publishers, but very few with your intelligence and integrity. To Richard Mintzer, who has worked with me, enabling me to refine and organize my thoughts, you have been an immeasurable help. You are able to shift through my ramblings and provide direction. Working with you has been a pleasure.

I would also like to thank Shirley, who is my right and left hand, and the rest of my wonderful office staff at the Irlen Institute International HQ. I extend my gratitude for keeping me sane and helping me laugh when I wanted to cry. I could not ask for a finer group of individuals with whom to share my days.

To my husband, who has survived having the lights turned on at all hours of the night so that I could write down my thoughts—which, otherwise, would have been gone by morning. To my daughter Sandy and granddaughter Molly who will continue on this journey long after I am gone. This journey may be a combination of hills and valleys, but the ability to change lives is well worth the effort.

I am thankful to have changed the lives of so many, and look forward to the opportunity to help so many more.

A Note on Gender

When writing this book, I was determined to fairly reference both males and females. In general, when a third-person pronoun is necessary, it is unbiased and conscientious to use "he or she" and "his or her." But that phrasing can be lengthy and awkward when employed repeatedly throughout paragraphs. So, I decided to alternate gendered personal pronouns according to chapter. The odd-numbered chapters use masculine pronouns, while the even-numbered chapters use feminine pronouns. I hope this makes the writing both respectful and easy to read.

Preface

At last, I am very pleased to have a second book in which to share my information about the Irlen Method. My first book, *Reading by the Colors*, was published way back in 1991. *Reading by the Colors* successfully introduced the method of reading with colored filters to improve the often unidentified Scotopic Sensitivity Syndrome, now known as Irlen Syndrome.

The first book, however, achieved much more than simply introducing Irlen Syndrome. It revealed that reading problems go beyond phonics and can be caused by a perceptual disorder, explaining that the Irlen Method provides clear and stable print on the page, which is a basic building block for successful reading. The book introduced perceptual problems that dealt with the brain and how it responded to processing material from the printed page. After some initial skepticism, we were met with positive responses from around the world. A decade of hard work paid off as we found that people all over, from America to Australia, who had struggled to read were no longer struggling thanks to our efforts. I was, and still am, very proud that we were able to accomplish more than we had initially anticipated, and I was excited to put it into book form.

Since the publication of the book in 1991, there have been numerous new developments on these topics. We have found that reading is just one of many activities where processing information can go awry. In an updated version of the 1991 book, published in 2005, I expanded the field to include information about how individuals with Attention Deficit Disorder (ADD) and Attention Deficit Hyperactivity Disorder (ADHD) are often being mislabeled. I explained that processing issues can be a problem not only for this population, but also for people with head injuries, autism, and an increasing number of other medical problems. The connection between the eyes and the brain and the ability to ingest and process the information from the printed page were also shown to be affected by such medical disorders.

The purpose of this book is to reintroduce Irlen Syndrome and the Irlen Method in order to catch readers up on how they came to be. However, its main purpose is to move forward, covering our new discoveries and developments in the field, as well as those made in the medical field. The book also examines the changes in the educational system and the manner in which children (and adults) today are labeled—and, very often, mislabeled—in a constant effort to group individuals into pre-established, often "trendy" categories. The sad result is that too many children who should be tested for Irlen Syndrome are not because Irlen Syndrome does not show up on "standardized tests." As a result of this, many undiagnosed children mature into undiagnosed adults. The problems they experienced as children do not fade away. The earlier a person is tested for Irlen Syndrome, the better.

Helen Irlen

Introduction

It's been a long time since my first book, *Reading by the Colors*. So much has changed, and there have been so many new revelations. We now understand that brain-based difficulties give people with Irlen Syndrome a unique way of seeing the world. In this book, I cover the broad spectrum, from the early days of research with struggling readers to the latest findings that have helped so many individuals with symptoms caused by illnesses and injuries.

The book begins by discussing an innovative approach to help those struggling with perceptual processing problems. I create an awareness of the various difficulties that result from this one underlying and, often, unidentified root cause. One method—the Irlen Method—offers a solution.

This book explains how having a problem processing visual information can cause physical symptoms and fragmented vision that affects attention, concentration, and performance for many with reading difficulties, as well as those with learning disabilities, dyslexia, ADD, ADHD, autism, and those with certain medical and psychological conditions. Regardless of whether or not you or your child have been diagnosed as having a problem— and regardless of the diagnosis—an inability of the brain to accurately process visual information may be the root cause, and Irlen Method may be the solution.

The Irlen Method has been able to help children and adults who come in a variety of sizes, shapes, and ages and who have a wide variety of diagnoses. Many people wonder how one method can be the solution for so many different problems. There is a simple explanation: All of these problems have one root cause—the brain's inability to correctly process visual information.

There is an old saying, "You shouldn't comment on what I am saying until you have lived life through my eyes." This is particularly true for the millions of children and adults who have been helped by the Irlen Method. No one knows what anyone else is seeing or feeling, nor do those who have processing difficulties understand that what they see or feel is different from what other people see or feel. Some of their stories are included in this book so that you can understand the personal challenges these people experience and the changes that the Irlen Method has made to each of their lives.

As with any other method, the Irlen Method has faced—and still sometimes faces—a handful of cynics. Most often, these cynics are professionals who do not personally suffer from any of the issues my clients face. However, critics want more than personal stories of success, and with that in mind, I have included the results of brain studies that have established the link between the Irlen Method and improving the brain's ability to accurately process information.

There are four categories of people who can be helped by the Irlen Method, all of whom are discussed in this book. They are:

- People who have an inherited predisposition

- People who acquired this problem as a result of some medical condition or head injury

- People who have been misdiagnosed with other conditions

- People who are suffering from a disability without any current known cause, such as autism.

The first group, people who have Irlen Syndrome, are born with an inherited predisposition to having sensitivity to certain environmental stimuli. For these individuals, the environments that are the most stressful are the classroom and workplace, where fluorescent lighting, whiteboards, textbooks, computer screens, and the need to focus and stay focused for long periods of time are dominant. This book will help you to identify whether you, or a loved one, have a reading or learning problem related to Irlen Syndrome.

The second group of individuals that the Irlen Method can help includes those who, as a result of a wide variety of medical conditions or a head injury, have acquired difficulties processing visual information. Their problems and symptoms are not life-threatening and do not respond to medical attention. Therefore, if reported, they are usually dismissed and no recommendations are made. However, these symptoms do create problems dealing with the environment on a day-to-day basis. This book will help you identify if you, or your child, are silently suffering with symptoms that can be resolved by the Irlen Method, regardless of the medical condition.

The third group discussed in this book includes people who have been misdiagnosed. For many children and adults with learning disabilities, dyslexia, ADD, ADHD, and certain psychological problems—such as anxiety, depression, panic disorders, and even agoraphobia—the root cause of their difficulties is being overlooked. Their symptoms are thought to have an entirely different cause, which can lead to years of frustration.

The final group discussed in this book is people who suffer from either inherited or acquired Irlen symptoms. Similar to the others discussed in the book, the symptoms of sensory sensitivity and sensory overload can be addressed with the Irlen Method for this group, including those with autism spectrum disorders. Although not a cure for this population, in some cases the Irlen Method can alleviate some of their difficulties. For me, the saddest part of not recognizing the importance of reducing sensory overload for this population is the resulting chaotic world in which they continue to live. The symptoms caused by sensory overload are more severe for those on the autism spectrum than for any of the other populations discussed in this book, an issue you will learn more about in Chapter 10 (page 129).

It goes without saying that for all of the populations discussed, only some individuals will be able to be helped. There are various self-tests included throughout this book to help you identify if you or your child are one of the lucky ones. The changes that occur with the Irlen Method can be immediate and life-changing. Since Irlen Syndrome is only a piece of the puzzle, and since the Irlen Method can help only certain individuals, Appendix A (page 176) describes other underlying and silent root causes for difficulties with attention, concentration, and performance, along with providing a variety of recommendations for how individuals who fall into these categories can be helped.

In certain cases, such as with certain academic difficulties, neither the Irlen Method nor any other method can remove the learning barrier. In recognition of the many other pieces of the puzzle and wanting to provide your child with the greatest likelihood for success, an Appendix (page 184) of strategies for success is also included, featuring suggestions for the struggling learner. This helps you become the expert and lets you determine the strategies that are best suited to your, or your child's, learning style.

For parents, another major topic of my book is advocating for your child. For those of you who are parents, you will understand what I mean when I say that sometimes we need to play detective and dig deep before discovering the pot of gold. This means starting at the top with the behaviors your child exhibits. However, behaviors do not tell you the cause. You need to dig down in order to uncover the cause of the behaviors. In this book, you will find many possible underlying reasons for the behaviors your child exhibits. For some, Irlen Syndrome may be the cause, but I encourage you to explore all the different possibilities I present—you never know which one will fit best.

Also in the pages you are about to read, I hope to create an awareness of problems and symptoms that are often deemed unimportant or insignificant. The widely accepted concept that everyone sees the exact same thing when looking at a printed page is wrong, and has been proven wrong through research and numerous tests. Whether the problem is hereditary or caused by any number of factors, including illness or injury, this very real processing problem affects people worldwide.

Therefore, if you are a parent, an educator, or an individual working hard to process information on the printed page; if you are struggling with light sensitivity or have trouble with depth perception, this book is for you. It is for everyone who is searching for answers, everyone who is frustrated and trying to determine why processing sensory information is so difficult, and everyone who is discouraged by the limited options offered by the educational, medical, and/or bureaucratic systems—none of which are coming up with sufficient answers or solutions, and in most cases are not even providing adequate testing to do so. The hope is that this book will provide another avenue that you can explore to help your child, your student, and/or yourself.

In short, I wrote this book so individuals would know that the Irlen Method is available and can help the many ongoing symptoms and challenges they face. My wish is for as many children and adults as possible to enjoy living the best life they possibly can. The more pieces of the puzzle that can be identified and addressed, the closer we are to achieving this goal.

It is time for you to learn about the story of Irlen Syndrome and how far it has come over the past two decades.

1

From the Beginning

"Colors for My Eyes"

by Victoria Ashley Bonacquista

Before I had my colors,
I really scared my mother,
When my eyes were bad, it really made
  me sad.
The letters would wiggle and jiggle,
  jump and bump.
They looked like they were in a lump.
Then mom took pieces of colored plastic
  and covered the letters.
Then my words would not spin.
When I put the colors on my face,
  the words honestly stayed in place.
I am as happy as can be.
When I read with my colors on,
  I can see.

What this lovely poem, written by a young girl, is referring to is the Irlen Method of wearing colored filters to make reading possible. It is this kind of enthusiastic response that makes my work so very rewarding.

For Victoria, reading—which was once a dreaded activity—is now a welcome part of daily life. The same holds true for numerous corporate leaders, lawyers and other professionals, both in the United States and around the globe. For years these people could not understand why read-

Figure 1.1. Eye of the Storm. Move back and forth while looking at the image, and it should appear to move.

ing was so difficult. Now they have found that there is a solution available so they no longer have to find ways to work around, or try to hide, their difficulties. Many of these same individuals—who were tagged with any number of labels from general learning disabilities to attention deficit disorder—now have a sense of newfound freedom that comes from having removed the shackles that were slowing them down and making them feel stupid or not as intelligent as their peers. In many cases, these people had never even realized there was a problem until they found out that they had Irlen Syndrome.

It may seem odd to imagine that some people could go months, or even years, without realizing they have a problem, but it is quite possible. You see, Irlen Syndrome is not a vision disorder. Nor is it your typical reading problem. It is not ADD, ADHD, or a behaviorial problem. Irlen Syndrome is a perceptual dysfunction that affects the processing of information as it passes from the eyes to the brain. When you read—whether from a printed page, a computer screen, or other surface—the eyes take in the words or information. It is the brain that processes the information. However, it is not uncommon for the brain to translate items differently than they appear. For example, if you look at an optical illusion, you will see how the pictures can appear to move, change, or appear to have colors when they do not (see Figures 1.1, 1.2, and 1.3). Clearly it is not the eyes but rather the brain that causes the illusions.

We can also change the way the brain perceives information by using something as simple as color. Have you ever watched a 3-D movie wearing colored 3-D glasses? When you take the glasses off, you will see the difference the colored lenses made on the way your brain interpreted the information on the screen. The colored lenses on 3-D glasses make the action jump off the screen; yet when you take them off, the movie is two-dimensional—and very blurry. They change the way your brain perceives what is on the screen.

Figure 1.2. **Rotating Spiral Snakes.** The circles appear to spiral.

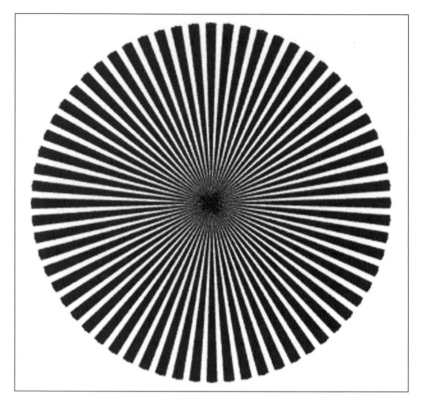

Figure 1.3. Shimmering Optical Illusion. Look into the center of this spiral. You should start to see white lines radiating out from the center, and you may even see white flashes and different colors.

The concept of Irlen Syndrome is similar to optical illusions and 3-D movies. When dealing with Irlen Syndrome, the letters on the printed page (or other surface) are perceived as moving or unstable in some manner. For many people, this dysfunction is hereditary. For others, Irlen-like symptoms may have been caused by injury or illness. (Irlen-like symptoms will be discussed in later chapters of the book.)

Typically, the processing problem for those with Irlen Syndrome involves the intake of light. Have you ever tried to read something written on a glossy piece of paper under a bright light but couldn't do so because of the way the light hit the paper? Later, if you read from the same piece of paper under diffused lighting, it may have been easier to see. You didn't change the words, nor did your eyesight change. However, you read the words more easily under one light as opposed to the other. This is because perception for many people can be altered by the manner in which they take in light. Again, this is an example of the transmission from the eyes to the brain. Remember, the eye-to-brain connection is very significant (see the inset on page 10). Unfortunately, this connection does not generate sufficient attention in the educational and medical fields. Typically, if someone has trouble reading, the cause is assumed to be either:

- A visual problem that needs to be corrected with glasses, or

- Difficulty learning the basic reading skills and phonics, or not having enough practice to achieve the flow and fluency needed for comprehension.

It has become evident from years of research that not everyone sees letters and words in the same manner, with the same spacing, or even as recognizable letters. Some people see letters jumping around on the page, dancing or swirling, while others see the words all jumbled together. This, in essence, is Irlen Syndrome. For the numerous people who have this issue, there is good news because we have found a solution to this very real (and often overlooked) problem.

To put everything into perspective, the best place to start is at the beginning. So, let's take a look back at how it all began, including how Irlen Syndrome was first discovered and what we have since learned.

WORKING IN THE SCHOOLS

During the 1970s, when I was working as a school psychologist in a Southern California school district, I met with numerous children, some briefly and many for long periods of time. My job was to get to the root of the problems that each individual student was affected by. For some, it was the usual peer pressure; while, for others, there were clearly issues at home that were manifesting in the classroom.

Then there were the students who were sent to me with learning problems. Of course, "learning disabilities," as they came to be known, spanned a very large spectrum. While some issues were short-term and easily solved with some degree of intervention and/or special education, other problems persisted. Being that I was in a small school district, I was able to see many of these children grow up, struggling in the early grades and, sadly, continuing to struggle through middle school and high school. Great frustration would take its toll on some of these students, who either dropped out of school or tried to mask their frustration by

Human Eye/Brain

The human eye is a light-sensitive organ of vision. The parts of the eye work together to change visible electromagnetic light energy into electrochemical energy within the brain. Visual perception, otherwise known as what you see, is the result of the complex interaction between the eye and the brain. The system is remarkable, but it is not perfect. Let's first take a closer look at the human eye.

The sclera is a tough, white tissue layer that covers the outside of the eyeball, and the cornea is a transparent membrane that interrupts the sclera in the front of the eye, forming a slight bulge in the eyeball over the pupil. The cornea, which is thicker in the center, serves as an outer lens to magnify images. Behind the cornea is the pupil, the opening through which light enters the eye. Surrounding the pupil is the iris, a pigmented tissue that acts like a circular diaphragm, widening and constricting to adjust the amount of light that enters the pupil. Behind the pupil is the lens, which focuses the light that enters through the pupil and transmits an inverted and reversed image onto the retina. Attached to the transparent and flexible lens are ciliary muscles. These muscles work to adjust the lens in order to clearly focus images onto the retina. The cells of the retina begin the journey along the visual pathway through the brain.[1] This is the beginning of the process that allows you to see. To find answers about the theoretical basis for Irlen Syndrome, researchers are studying how the brain processes visual information.

In 2003, at the Forty-Fifth Annual Conference of the International Military Testing Association in Pensacola, Florida, Susann Krouse and James H. Irvine presented a report on "Perceptual Dyslexia—also known as Irlen Syndrome." They discussed the numerous studies of this visual-perceptual disorder that have been conducted. The general consensus is that Scotopic Sensitivity Syndrome (now known as Irlen Syndrome) affects the way the visual pathways carry messages from the eye to the brain.

It is theorized that when the receptor fields do not sum to unity, the pathways are affected, causing the magnocellular impulses to be slowed, so only partial perception occurs. This results in words that blur, fuse, or seem to jump off the page (Newman, 1998). Individualized colored filters seem to return the balance between the two processing systems, preventing this overlapping (Robinson, 1994). The colored overlays and filters cut down or eliminate the perceptual problem by screening out the wavelengths of light troublesome to the individual. Studies of both the long- and short-term efficacy of the transparencies and filters have shown that they do, indeed, provide benefits . . . [2]

resorting to drugs or alcohol. After all, growing up struggling to read and comprehend information made these children feel stupid or as if they were outcasts. Often they were told that they weren't trying hard enough or that they needed to work harder. Those who tried harder were that much more disillusioned, because no matter how hard they worked, they still lagged behind. Reading was still a nightmarish process. As a result, these children had serious confidence problems that manifested themselves in various ways.

If growing up in this manner wasn't bad enough, many of these children were told that if they practiced and worked hard, their problems would go away. That was one of the overriding themes of the 1970s—that adults no longer had reading or learning difficulties. But it was the students with academic difficulties who disappeared or dropped out of the educational system as soon as possible. Unfortunately, I was seeing children go from childhood to adulthood with no change occurring. They grew to be discouraged by the system, as did I.

Frustration

While working in the school system, I could see frustration arising from the parents of these struggling students. They were frustrated with the school system, which did not recognize that their children had problems because they seemed to be performing "adequately." And they were frustrated because they, as parents, were very aware of how much extra effort, energy, and time it was taking their children to complete their schoolwork. The schools did not see how long and hard their children worked on completing homework and were unaware of the fact that it might take these students three hours to do a one-hour homework assignment.

What made it worse was that even if the parents did get the school to recognize that a problem existed, there was then a very long delay in getting the child tested due to paperwork, funding, and scheduling issues. Once the child was finally tested, there were no signs of progress for some—even if special help was administered.

The final level of frustration, which parents did not even communicate to the schools, was that they were very aware that the concept of their children outgrowing this problem was a fallacy. They knew it would not just "go away" because many of them had suffered silently with their own reading problems for years and continued to do so well into adulthood. These parents knew, deep down inside, that this was a problem their children would not outgrow.

During this time, I was also conducting parent groups for the parents of children with reading and learning difficulties, so I heard their concerns loud and clear. I heard their anger with the system and their concern that for every year this continued for a given child, he would be losing out on more education. "We need to do something and nothing is getting done!" was a familiar cry from the parents.

I would also hear from teachers after I tested a child and was unable to identify the problem. "I don't know how your test cannot show that there's a problem," teachers would say. "Come into my classroom and watch this child and you'll see that this child can't perform." I believed the teachers and I believed the parents, but at the same time I was getting aggravated because nothing was showing up on the tests. Thus, I could not determine a concrete plan of action. I also became very aware of the fact that even if I was able to get a child help through special education, it didn't necessarily mean he got any better. In fact, many of these children stayed in special education and never returned to regular classrooms.

All of these factors made me realize that something different needed to be done. We needed to step back and look at the bigger picture. I began to question the entire system and the process we were using. What was it that we were not doing? Was standardized testing enough? Were we identifying all of the problems that were out there, or did we need to do something in addition to the testing in order to detect other problems? As a school psychologist, I used the standardized psycho-educational battery of tests used to identify a child as having a learning disability. This included IQ testing, achievement testing, and tests for processing difficulties. Later I discovered that these tests were not picking up the type of processing problems related to Irlen Syndrome, so most of these children were simply falling through the cracks without ever discovering solutions to their problems.

Children Stop Reporting

The only other testing that was done by the schools was for vision and hearing. Usually, when students had reading problems or teachers felt that there was a difficulty seeing, a visual examination was recommended by the school nurse. If a problem was detected, glasses were prescribed. It was still assumed that once a child was given glasses, all his problems with "seeing" would go away. This was not always the case.

What did go away, however, was the reporting. When children reported that reading gave them headaches, their complaints were dismissed. So the children stopped reporting the headaches. Once schools stopped hearing about headaches, it was assumed that the headaches had gone away. Sadly, this was not the case.

Another issue with reporting was that some suffering students did not even realize they were suffering. For example, a child who always gets a headache from reading might assume this is the norm. He would likely also assume that all people get headaches if they read for awhile. I'll never forget the time I asked an adult client why she didn't tell anyone that she got a headache from reading. She looked at me with a puzzled expression and responded, "I didn't know I was supposed to. Don't most people get a headache if they read long enough?" If a person—adult or child—doesn't know any better, there is a high likelihood he won't report a problem.

SEARCHING FOR RESULTS

By the start of the 1980s, the long-standing concept that children would outgrow reading problems and learning disabilities was finally replaced with acceptance that learning and reading problems can continue on into adulthood. This realization led to the proliferation of programs for adults with learning disabilities at community colleges and universities throughout the United States. One such program was launched in 1981 at a California State University near my home. I was asked to be the coordinator of the program, which would contain a research component to determine why these adult students were still struggling. Twenty years prior, as an undergraduate at Cornell University, I had been a research assistant. So I was excited about the opportunity to finally put my research background to use by seeking out solutions to the reading problems that persisted despite remediation and special education classes.

Having some latitude to set up my own process for studying those adult students who still had reading problems, I was able to look at various methodologies. First, I considered the differences between how testing is approached in education and in medicine. There's a philosophy in education that when you test someone, you get results and can then definitively say, "here's your problem," without asking the person being tested to provide any additional information, describe the problem, or even asking if the information is correct. However, when you look at the medical model of testing, a lot of self-reporting is used. For example, when you go to a physician, the first question you are typically asked is, "Can you tell me about your problem?" You're asked to explain your symptoms and what is bothering you. This kind of testing model is often ignored in the educational system. However, it was exactly the kind of model that I decided to apply in my research.

I decided I would work with an adult population that had ongoing reading problems affecting their ability to succeed in college. I would start by getting information directly from them. After all, none of the standardized tests were providing us with any answers. So, tapping into my research background, I chose to start at the source—the troubled readers themselves.

The Research Group

Today it is pretty standard for students coming out of high school—who have been provided with interventions and accommodations—to understand that similar help is also available at the college level. Back in the 1980s, however, it was not readily available. Such adult learning programs were new and innovative.

The initial thirty-five adult (eighteen and older) California State University students that I was set to work with came into this unique adult learning program because they were struggling academically. In some cases, they were on academic probation and were told that if they didn't join the program, they were at risk of failing and would be kicked out of the university. Upon entering the program (begrudgingly for most), the students knew that I was a school psychologist and that I did testing. They also knew that this was important because it could determine whether or not they could remain in, and make it through, college. It could ultimately determine their future career paths.

Most of these students were skeptical and even a bit jaded or cynical, sporting attitudes that nothing was going to help. They didn't really expect anything would come from the program because they had already tried so many things and poured their hearts into numerous futile efforts. So, from the start, I empathized with them and was careful not to promise anything. I let them know that first, I just wanted to start a dialogue. Immediately their attitudes changed. Their expectations didn't increase by much, but they were thrilled to have somebody who would actually listen to them and let them explain what was going on. The students were all tired of people labeling them or telling them what their problems were. As a result of the educational model of testing, none of the students ever had any say in the testing process. They were forced to follow along like rats in a maze. I was going to actually talk to them and hear them out. This was a first for almost all of the thirty-five students.

From our dialogue, reading was not the only area these students were struggling in. We found other areas that nobody had ever even asked them about but that seemed to be related to their difficulties with learning, attention, and performance. These areas, that were also identified and addressed, will be discussed later on in this book (see Appendix A on page 176).

Digging Deeper

It was then time to try to figure out exactly what was at the root of the reading problems for the struggling students. Our hope was to find an answer and extend the solution to struggling readers of all ages—especially children, who need solutions before the problem continues to go ignored for years. It made sense to learn what questions to ask and how to ask the questions in the right manner from adults who were still struggling. Since we were also embarking on brand new research, we knew it might take a considerable amount of time. I didn't want to put children through another lengthy process if we had no idea what to expect as an outcome.

My research background taught me that if you wanted to do a comprehensive study of anything, you had to set up all of the parameters from the very beginning of the process and proceed slowly, step-by-step. So, I started with some very basic questions to set the stage.

When you read for awhile, are the words clear, stable, and is it comfortable?

That was my first question, simply to use as a basis to continue asking a series of questions that would follow. In my mind, it was almost like asking, "When you drive, do you start by sitting down in the driver's seat behind the steering wheel?" In other words, I thought the answer would be obvious. Much to my surprise, that first question was as far as I got. I had assumed that people who had problems seeing the words when reading had already corrected those problems with glasses or contact lenses. I needed to make sure that this was true. Instead, these adults reported that whether they wore glasses or had been told that they did not need glasses, the print did not stay clear or stable, and reading did not remain comfortable.

Even though my assumption was wrong, this simple question proved to be groundbreaking. Before me, nobody had ever asked these students about the actual process of seeing the words on the page and what they looked like. When I asked, the students told me that the words were moving around, that they were swirling, dancing, jumbled, or all bunched together. I was also told that as the students read, it got worse.

These responses absolutely floored me, so much so that I decided to set up a control group of graduate students who had no reported reading problems. The control group was made up of twenty-five graduate students between the ages of twenty-two and forty-five. I started by asking this group the same question I had asked the research group. When I got the kind of responses I'd expected, I asked a few more questions.

When you read, are the words clear, stable, and comfortable?
Yes.
Do you like to read for awhile?
Yes.
Is the print still clear, stable, and comfortable after five minutes of reading? After an hour of reading? After two hours of reading?

Yes, yes, and yes were the answers. The control group had no problems with moving, dancing, or swirling letters at all. The words were always clear and stable, and reading was comfortable for them no matter how long they read.

Could it actually be that we had connected with a problem that was bypassed by all the standard testing for learning disabilities? Had we discovered a problem that was not being detected by the visual examinations? Along with my team—which consisted of my own graduate assistants—I knew that we had discovered something unexpected and that we needed to explore it further.

Bringing in the Experts

It was at that point we decided to bring in a board of professionals to meet with and evaluate the thirty-five struggling adult readers. This board included optometrists, ophthalmologists, developmental optometrists, neurologists, psychologists, and reading specialists. We had helped the students become aware of what was actually going on and found a language in which they could finally describe their problems. Therefore, they were able to use the medical model of explaining their problems to the board of professionals who could evaluate them and, so we thought, find a cure.

The college students were individually evaluated by each of the professionals, who were told to make recommendations for treatment. The students explained that they saw letters moving, dancing, and swirling with words all jumbled together when they tried to read. They explained that they got headaches when they read and that their symptoms typically got worse the longer they read. Some of the students were provided glasses and a variety of others suggestions were implemented, but after a period of nine months, the thirty-five struggling readers returned to report that nothing had changed. In essence, much to my surprise, there were no treatments, therapies, or cures found. We were almost right back where we were nine months earlier, with the core group of individuals still suffering the same symptoms and still voicing the same complaints as they continued to struggle to read. However, we did learn that this was not an undiagnosed vision problem; therefore, glasses and vision exercises made no difference. Neither did medication or other interventions. These adults knew how to read and months of instruction and practice in various reading method did little to eliminate the root cause of their reading difficulties, their distortions, and their physical discomfort.

Once again, I was surprised at the results (or lack thereof). And once again, the research group was disappointed, a feeling they were all too familiar with. Even now, being able to express and describe the problems like never before, they were still not getting the help they needed.

Creating the Distortions

To get an idea of what this core group was actually seeing, we had them create, on paper, the way the written page appeared to them. For the first time, we were able to look at the distortions and see how these readers saw words on paper. We then copied the pages that this group created and gave them to the control group of graduate student readers and asked if they could read them. Once we did that, the graduate students were struggling to read much in the same manner as our core group of struggling readers had always done.

"Why would anybody in their right mind want to read like this?" several of the graduate students asked. The graduate students found themselves trying hard to get through a single page, much less page after page, with such distortions.

We then knew that we could create the distortions on paper and show how difficult it was to read in such a manner. I was able to create a problem for someone who could read without any difficulty by giving them a distortion. The obvious question remained. Could we make the distortions go away for these struggling readers?

Frostig Exercises

It was still in the early 1980s and we had made one major breakthrough—discovering the root cause of a certain type of reading problem that was neither phonics nor vision-based but was, instead, an issue of processing. Somewhere between the eye and the brain something was not being processed properly.

I began researching any and all methods I could find that had ever been used to help or improve either perceptual or reading problems. This led me to Frostig methods.

Austrian-born Marianne Frostig, who founded the Frostig Center in Pasadena, California, developed an approach for teaching children with specific learning disabilities. Frostig's approach stressed the necessity of an interdisciplinary and multidimensional diagnostic evaluation as a basis for planning an educational or therapeutic learning program for each child. She and her team developed standardized tests to assess the child's developmental status in movement (motor skills) and perception.

Frostig exercises include repeating tasks that are often done with young school children who have perceptual problems. The idea is to repeat the task over and over again until it gets easier. One such task is having two forms on paper with a tunnel drawn between them. The task is to draw a straight line through the tunnel from one item to the other without touching the lines on the sides of the tunnel (see Figure 1.4). Using the two groups, we did the exercises with our core group of readers and then repeated the same activities with the control group of proficient readers.

The core group of struggling readers could not do it, while the control group had no problem. In fact, the struggling readers complained

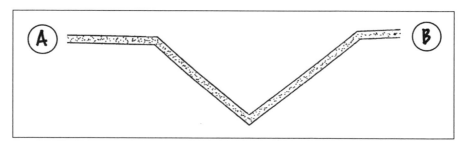

Figure 1.4. Frostig Exercise. When asked to draw a line through the tunnel (from A to B) without touching the tunnel sides, the core group of readers could not complete the task. The control group had no problem.

that it got more difficult as they continued to try because the lines were not staying still on the page. Some explained that they saw the lines moving up and down, while others said that the lines actually disappeared.

It appeared at this point that educational, therapeutic, repetitive, and other such learning tasks were not going to work for the struggling group of readers.

A COLORFUL AWAKENING

We had been working diligently for over a year with no real solution to speak of when we began exploring the dominant eye theory, one of the many theories we discovered while researching perceptual and reading problems. Popular in some sports, such as basketball and golf, the dominant eye theory, at that time, was also used to help with reading problems. Children who were struggling to read would be asked to put something over one eye to build dominance in the other. Since many children did not feel comfortable covering one eye, red and green glasses (one lens was red and one lens was green) were also used to make it easier for one eye to see and harder for the other. This was different than the Frostig exercises because it did not require any degree of practicing and repeating tasks at all—so much for the theory that practice makes perfect!

For our purposes, the group of struggling readers tried reading through the red and green glasses with a red overlay on the page. They reported it was easier to read, but just as easy as reading with only the red overlay, and definitely better than reading on the white page.

At last, something was making a difference! Needless to say, we were excited. Since we had found a possible solution to the problem, it was time to probe and try to find out exactly what was happening and why. All the students who had reported distortions when reading saw a difference when reading with the red overlay. For some, the color eliminated their distortions so that the words were clear and remained still, but for others, the red overlay only made a slight difference. Since this method worked for some but not as well for all of the students, we considered the idea that color might be an answer—but perhaps a different color would work for different people.

We went to the theater department at the university, where theatrical gels are used to change the color of lighting during a stage production, to get samples of other colored gels. These would prove to be helpful because they came in such a wide variety of colors.

The variety of colors worked. For the first time, thanks to the colored overlays, all of the struggling readers were able to see words on paper that were not jumping, swirling, dancing, or all jumbled together. They were excited, to say the least. Remember, these were adults who entered this program over a year earlier never expecting anything to happen or thinking that anything would change.

Initial Reactions

One woman, after reading with an overlay for the first time, looked up from the page and told me that it was like magic. Then she started laughing, then crying, because her feelings were so strong and so overwhelming. She had struggled to read for so long and was suddenly able to without such a great effort. "It's like you put seatbelts on the words," she told me. It was a great statement because for those who had witnessed letters and words running all over the page, they now appeared stable as if strapped in with seatbelts.

Another marvelous reaction came from a woman who was standing with a friend who did not have Irlen Syndrome (as the disorder came to be known). When we put the overlays down, she commented that it was like magic. Then, as many of us do when we experience something amazing, she wanted to share it with her friend. So the woman turned to her friend and said, "Here, look at this, isn't this absolutely wonderful?" Of course, the friend saw nothing different except the colored overlay over the words and responded, "I don't get it." Naturally, the friend could not share the excitement of suddenly being able to read through this overlay because she did not share the same reading issues as the woman she had came with.

Another woman who had graduated from college and was just about to embark on her post-graduate work told me how she had experienced a lot of pain and shame throughout her education. "I felt that I had earned my college degree by being a fake and that someday they would find out and take it away from me," she explained. She felt like she was using all kinds of strategies and tricks to understand the information she wasn't able to read like everyone else. In reality, she probably worked twice as hard as other students. With the overlays, she felt a sense of relief for the first time. She realized that she wasn't dumb and with that realization came the overwhelming joy of discovering who she really was. She, too, spent that first night after reading with the overlays laughing and crying.

Later, she went on to complete graduate school with a lot more ease than she completed college. In time, she became a school psychologist.

"More, Please!"

Following the initial breakthrough with the colored overlays, the thirty-five people from the core group kept journals for the rest of the semester to let me know how things were going. A majority of them feared that this "magical" solution to their reading problems would disappear as quickly as it had suddenly appeared. However, it did not. The colored overlays continued to help this group read as they never had before. The problem was now that these individuals had seen what it was like to read with stable letters on the page, letters wearing "seatbelts," so to speak, they wanted more. Several of them came to me and explained that now that the letters on the page remained still, they wanted to know if I could help them with the letters moving around on whiteboards or computer screens. As it turned out, it was not just letters on the printed page that swirled and danced around, but letters on other surfaces as well. Numbers, math signs, and musical notes also caused problems. Now that the students had seen the difference on paper, they were able to express clearly what they were experiencing in other areas as well. "Can you fix this too?" and "Can you make this better?" were popular questions I was receiving, and as a psychologist (and a mom), my somewhat naïve response was, "Of course I'll try to make it better for you."

The next step was to transfer the overlays into something wearable, and the obvious solution was colored glasses. After all, if color was helping with the words on the page, then the logical assumption was that it would also work with the words on whiteboards or computer screens as well as with numbers and musical notes. Ultimately, that assumption was correct. However, what floored me was that the color of the overlay that helped with reading the page was not helping when worn as colored glasses. So, once again, we set out on a mission to determine which color (or combination of colors) when worn as glasses would benefit these people in other areas.

In some instances, we needed to combine as many as five or six different colors into one set of lenses. It was a rather technical process because of the multitude of possible colors and variations you find when you look across the spectral band. You don't have just red, you have green-red, blue-red, and so on, and we needed to find the best variation of the color to help each person. As we created lenses of different colors and of different densities, it was the adults (the core group) who provided the feedback on what worked and how well it worked. Eventually, we were able to come up with a method of testing to determine the needed colors, and finally we started providing filtered glasses to our group of adults with Irlen Syndrome. Now, with their individually-determined Irlen Filters, the people in the core group were relaying positive changes when looking at whiteboards, computer screens, and so on.

Shortly afterwards, word of what we were doing started spreading very quickly, and our initial group of 35 had grown to 1,050 simply by word of mouth—we were not marketing or promoting our findings. We were still in the study and research phase because, quite honestly, we didn't know if this change would last over time. While I did not want to sound negative to this group of people, I also could provide no guarantees of lasting results.

Long-Term Findings

In an effort to see if the filters could work their magic over time, we began monitoring the individuals to see if words and letters continued to stay still as a result of the filters. It was important that we continued to see the same positive results, which is why we did not want our findings to go "mainstream" or present our findings to the mass public too soon. To this day, even with worldwide testing and distribution of the Irlen Filters, we are still keeping track of the original research group, most whom have been wearing their filters for over twenty-five years now.

After about three years, we were clearly able to differentiate between who we could and who we could not help. Having established a screening system, we knew exactly what to look for and what questions to ask, so we finally began screening children. We finally knew all the various types of distortions, and we were able to anticipate hearing about them in response to our questions. We knew that we were clearly not looking at developmental or vision-related issues. The children were replying with the same answers, replicating those the adults had been providing during the three years of the study.

Since our group of 1,050 was made up of primarily young adults in college or at the post-graduate levels, we were not yet able to study issues related to heredity. However, independent research studies later confirmed theories that Irlen Syndrome is indeed hereditary. I would later meet families who had Irlen Syndrome passed down from one generation to the next.

GOING PUBLIC

It was halfway around the world—in the land down under—that the story of our findings first hit the public airways, thanks to an Australian journalist who was visiting the United States. The Australian version of *60 Minutes* did a story on our findings and received a tremendous response. Before I knew it, I was off to Australia to do interviews for a very receptive audience. Soon, New Zealand and Great Britain followed with major news stories that also resulted in an influx of calls and letters. However, it was not until 1988 that *60 Minutes* here in the United States aired the story "Reading by the Colors," which drew an avalanche of phone calls and letters from U.S. residents. Some 10,000 people had already been helped by Irlen Filters (sometimes referred to as Irlen Spectral Filters) in other parts of the world, and thousands more in the United States wanted to be screened for Irlen Syndrome.

Plenty of newspaper articles followed—many wanted to share their good fortune with others and, as a group, they became very strong advocates. A story soon appeared in *National Geographic*, lending even more creditability to our discovery. Pretty soon, Irlen Syndrome and Irlen Filters were popping up in all sorts of places, from the *Sally Jesse Raphael Show* where Raphael's guest, the late Margaux Hemingway, wore her Irlen Filters on the show and discussed their impact on her life, to episodes of the soap opera *General Hospital* in 1995. At the time, *General Hospital* was one of the most watched soaps on television. One of the characters, Stone, communicated to his psychologist that he was having difficulties reading. The psychologist informed Stone about the Irlen Method and had Stone try to read with colored overlays, which were effective, and Stone ended up getting a pair of Irlen Filters.

Much to my surprise, even some romance novels (*Walking on Air* by Casey Roberts and *Wild About a Texan* by Jan Hudson) worked Irlen Syndrome and the Irlen Filters into their storylines.

At that point, I was surprised by the sheer number of people contacting me asking for help; and I realized that I would need to train others, not just in the United States but around the world. The initial research project, which had helped thirty-five college students, had grown to be able to help so many more people, much larger in scope than I had ever anticipated.

We were providing a life-changing experience for those who came to see us. People who found reading to be challenging, frustrating, and exhausting were able to join the millions of others who enjoy reading.

At this time, which was around the early 1990s, more independent research was being done in various parts of the world, corroborating our findings and making additional discoveries. These research studies, often done with large groups made up of adults and children, were significant because they verified once again that there were changes occurring with comprehension, accuracy, and reading rate. The research was also showing that this was a long-term problem that had existed in many adults since childhood, and that we had found a long-term solution. In addition, we also had a whole contingency of people who got involved in their own independent research because they had become interested in the theory behind why color worked. That gave Irlen a theoretical basis, which was verified by brain research. And, as anyone in the scientific community knows, you need a theoretical basis and evidence from lots of research by others to make your discovery that much more credible, because research from other scientists and research that yields similar outcomes validate your findings and show that you are not the only one getting such results. Of course, I was elated that researchers were supporting my work—but for me, the most credibility came from the fact that adults and children, like the one who wrote the poem at the start of this chapter, were able to read without struggling.

CONCLUSION

We set out on a mission to try to solve problems we knew nothing about. It was obvious that testing and methods of remediation worked for some, but not all. Therefore, I needed to ask different questions in order to find different answers—if you don't ask, you don't find out. By asking simple questions that had never been asked in this specific way before, I heard things that had not been heard before. The people who had the problem helped by supplying the missing pieces of the reading puzzle by explaining what it was like for them to read. Simple questions opened a floodgate of marvelous answers, and Irlen Syndrome was eventually found to be able to help not just a few, but many who struggled with reading.

Yes, we had made a breakthrough, and we were elated. And yet, despite all the progress we had made, an uphill battle was lying ahead.

In the next chapter, you will learn about the roadblocks we faced as we fought to defend the Irlen Method against criticism from all angles. It was a tough fight, but we prevailed, continuing on to establish the Irlen Method and prove to everyone that we were here to stay.

2

Establishing the Irlen Method and Running Up Against Roadblocks

> "I am quite passionate about the Irlen Method. It feels good to be able to give parents a real solution instead of the usual negative reports to parents of students with learning difficulties. The joy, satisfaction, and gratitude that most parents have expressed when their kids are identified with Irlen are very rewarding. Many of these parents have had years of shaking heads and finding no solutions to their problems, and I have personally found that very frustrating and depressing."
>
> —CHRIS, TEACHER AND IRLEN SCREENER

When leaving this message, Chris wanted to share the wonderful feeling of being able to make a significant difference in the life of a child, which can be a very rewarding feeling. Unfortunately, because of the many obstacles and the resistance that has been placed in our way over the past twenty years, many parents, teachers, and children have not been able to share these wonderful moments.

Skepticism and mistrust of a new concept have not only been directed toward Irlen Syndrome, but toward all new and innovative ideas and discoveries, whether in medicine, education, or other fields. Therefore, it stands to reason that we faced tough scrutiny.

PROVING OURSELVES

New methodologies, new ideas, and new inventions all need to pass muster, so to speak, and I respect that. Professionals in nearly any field will challenge anything that is new and unfamiliar. They will put new concepts to the test to see if there is any existing value. After all, for every successful invention or new methodology, there are many trials that simply do not work or make only a small difference, while costing money that could be better spent on more traditional approaches. I fully expected challenges in the late 1980s and early 1990s when the Irlen Method was new; and, to some degree, I'm not surprised when questions are still raised today. It's part of the process; and, quite frankly, if someone had come to me twenty-five years ago with the concept of Irlen Filters, I too would have asked numerous questions before accepting that the problem was real and that color was a means of resolving the processing problems underlying certain types of reading and learning difficulties.

One of the early arguments I needed to refute was that Irlen Filters were only a placebo and the changes would not last. This was difficult to argue early on. However, over the years we have been able to document that children and adults who continue to wear their Irlen Filters continue to benefit from them. One research study followed the continued use and progress of Irlen Filter wearers over a six-year period, proving that long-term use was, in fact, beneficial.[1] We have gathered proof that this is not a short-term solution or a placebo effect. After all, could hundreds of thousands of children and adults all have the same placebo affect?

Another criticism the Irlen Method faced was that I did all of the research myself. Furthermore, some people said that all in all, there was little research done on the topic. Twenty years of independent research studies support our data showing the benefits of the Irlen Method and that this condition exists worldwide. The studies were completely independent from the others, so it was not even an enclave of researchers in a single community, much less all done by myself. In fact, research was done on three continents.

There were also the concerns by various state boards that the Irlen Method was not recognizing the importance of standard eye exams and was being used instead of regular eye glasses. However, before a child or adult is tested for Irlen Syndrome, a visual exam and any recommended correction must be in place. The Irlen Method doesn't replace a visual examination or glasses, but glasses cannot correct the processing problems those with Irlen Syndrome face. One of the reasons why we asked ophthalmologists, optometrists, developmental optometrists, psychologists, neurologists, and other professionals to evaluate and treat our initial study group was to see if any of them, using their skills and expertise, could find a solution for the problem since they were the experts in these fields. Of course, I was also fully expecting one of these professional groups would be able to provide a solution for this perplexing problem. As discussed, that did not happen.

In 1990 I was investigated for a year. The district attorney's office even sent an investigator who, while undercover, went through the testing process as a "client." At the end of the testing, he revealed his real purpose for being there. He then thanked everyone on the staff for being so professional and informed us that if he ever had a child who had this type of problem, he would bring her to the Irlen Institute for an evaluation. He was extremely supportive.

In the end, we cleared each and every hurdle along the way to the present day. We continued to show that the Irlen Method is not the practice of optometry, medicine, a placebo, or a method for teaching reading skills. What we achieved is a way to solve a specific processing problem that makes it difficult for some children—and adults—to learn to use their reading and other academic skills.

IRLEN SYNDROME IS NOT A LEARNING DISABILITY

It's important to mention that not all children with Irlen Syndrome have a learning disability (LD). Many children who suffer from Irlen Syndrome are bright and gifted. Additionally, not all children who have been diagnosed with or are suspected of having a learning disability can be helped by the Irlen Method.

Unfortunately, only those with a specific type of processing problem will benefit from the Irlen Method. As with many problems, a child with Irlen Syndrome can be mislabeled as having a learning disability because she has been struggling to see words and numbers on the page. In some cases, Irlen Syndrome may only be one of many problems the child faces; and even if it is corrected, she may still struggle with learning and need special education services. This was another criticism we faced over the years—that Irlen Filters would prevent a child from receiving the remedial instruction she needed. However, we never professed that the Irlen Method was a method of instruction; instead, we promoted that it was designed to rectify processing issues that can prevent a child from being able to learn or use her skills to the best of her ability.

As for learning disabilities in general, there is no single, clear, and widely accepted definition of what "learning disabilities" are. However, there are now at least twelve definitions with a few areas of commonality or areas in which everyone seems to agree. Those commonalities are:

- Children with learning disabilities are not a homogeneous group and exhibit a wide range of different problems. Difficulties can include problems with reading, writing, spelling, mathematics, comprehension, spoken language, listening, or reasoning.

- Discrepancies exist between a child's potential for learning and what is actually learned.

- Learning disabilities often run in families.

- Learning disabilities should not be confused with other disabilities, such as mental retardation, autism, deafness, blindness, attention deficit hyperactivity disorder (ADHD), and behavioral disorders. None of these conditions are learning disabilities, but individuals with these problems do qualify for special services. Many children with these problems have learning disabilities as well.

- The learning disabled have difficulties with academic achievement and progress.

Remember, the term "learning disability" is a label for a group of heterogeneous problems. It is just a diagnostic category that does not tell you anything about the type (or types) of problems an adult or child is coping with. The "learning disability" label also does not tell you the cause or the specific ways to deal with the problems. For parents, all that the label can provide is a guarantee that if your child qualifies, she will receive special services consisting of RSP (Resource Specialist Program), self-contained classroom placement, or additional help in the classroom from an individual specially trained in the field. Unfortunately, the teachers or special education workers helping these children are often working in the dark, making assumptions about what type of help is required.

It is very common, when dealing with special education, to believe that the same methods will work for all students labeled with learning disorders. This provides a "one-size-fits-all" type of program, when clearly learning disabilities cover a combination of different problems, different learning styles, and different processing difficulties. Special education teachers basically provide remedial instruction, often using the same teaching methods as mainstream teachers. This is essentially doing more of the same in a smaller setting, which doesn't result in change when the problem is a processing issue like Irlen Syndrome. As discussed, children with Irlen Syndrome do not benefit from repeating skills over and over because the problem is a barrier—preventing them from being able to clearly process information, no matter how many times they see it.

The myth in the educational system has been, and still is, that repetition and instruction will take care of all of the problems. In reality, however, if you don't find the underlying problem, you won't make progress—even with good instruction or repetition.

"Formal" Testing

To determine a learning disability, formal and informal test scores are used along with health and developmental information, educational and medical histories, previous records, teacher reports, and interviews with teachers and parents. The information obtained is used to assess the child's ability to succeed in school. Additional testing may include assessment of social, emotional, and behavioral factors. Academic performance is assessed using standardized instruments to measure whether or not the child is making adequate progress. In the past and even today, many districts require the child to be at least two years behind grade level in one or more academic areas in order to be eligible for special education services.

While this sounds very professional and comprehensive, there are problems in making a clear determination. Testing has limitations and often misses children who are truly struggling and need special help. Tests measure a small sample of a person's repertoire during a limited period of time. You need to understand that how well a student performs during testing—and the interpretation of said tests—is limited by a variety of factors including mood, motivation, physical wellbeing, and nerves. The most obvious factor that is overlooked is that the tests require each skill to be done for only a short time, whereas in class the child is required to perform the skills for a much longer period of time. Test scores are only an estimate of the child's ability or skills. Therefore, while they can be accurate, they can also be very deceptive. Even when test scores are combined with other information to determine whether the child qualifies for special education, many children who are struggling and should qualify for special services may be missed.

Finally, the language used in the learning disability reports is highly technical (not parent-friendly), and the interpretation is given in standard scores which is also difficult to comprehend. The reports provide parents with little understanding of their child's problems or what causes them, leaving most parents totally dependant on the school system to solve their child's problem.

For years, the identification of "learning disability" has been made by the school psychologist after testing. This method of testing is known as the discrepancy model, which has become the "gold standard" for labeling children, and even adults, with a learning disability. The consequence of creating such an arbitrary cutoff point is that the majority of people who have less severe learning difficulties are left to continue struggling and those with processing issues not identified by the tests—such as Irlen Syndrome—are completely missed.

In recent years, we have seen a shift in the field of special education. The criterion for determining who qualifies as learning disabled is changing as the tests are no longer standardized and the criteria for placement can vary. With the change, no longer are schools required to base determination of learning disabilities on a severe discrepancy between achievement and intellectual ability. This is a step in the right direction, allowing for a broader view of learning disabilities—potentially being able to identify far more children than in the past. However, many schools and school districts throughout the country are still using the discrepancy model.

To summarize, learning disabilities occur on a continuum, and only a few students who are in need of help will ever get identified. Therefore, the majority of children who are struggling in school are going to go unidentified and not receive the attention they need. To complicate matters, even if a child is identified and given special education, it does not mean the magic bullet or the cure has been discovered. This is not only true for Irlen Syndrome, but for various issues and problems that are missed by standardized testing.

So far, we have stressed the limitations of standardized testing. But parents, there are other reasons to have your child tested. Getting your child tested is often not easy, with many roadblocks placed in the way; but the sooner she is tested and receives special services, the better. If you suspect your child has a learning disability and want to have her tested, you will need to make the request for an assessment in writing and the school district must issue a plan within fifteen days of the receipt of your written request.

What is now even more frustrating is that the federal government finally recognizes that there is a need to look at processing issues and has given schools a directive to do so, but teachers and school psychologists are still not recognizing or testing for Irlen Syndrome—which is clearly a processing deficit. Those schools that do screen for students with Irlen Syndrome prior to testing for learning disabilities consistently find that over half of the students—when given a colored overlay—perform well enough in class that they no longer need to be tested for learning disabilities. If students who were tested for Irlen Syndrome and other processing difficulties were identified prior to "standardized" testing, this could save school districts a lot of money, while also preventing years of frustration for parents, students, and teachers. However, most teachers are not trained to identify this type of processing problem and, even more importantly, do not know what to do with this information; so they often ignore it and keep doing what is familiar and comfortable—continue teaching. Everyone knows the importance of early intervention, which can catch students with processing issues up front. After all, if the concept of making sure that everything a child sees is stable and comfortable is acted upon early, then she wouldn't have to struggle through years of school feeling bad about working hard and not being able to achieve, possibly dropping out of school, or deciding not to continue the educational process and go to college.

In addition to Irlen Syndrome, there are a number of other factors that can affect attention, concentration, and performance that are also missed entirely by the testing process, leaving parents discouraged and unsure of what they should do next. These issues, which include allergies and food reactions, can be found in the inset *Other Issues Not Detected by the Discrepancy Model*, on the next page, and in Appendix A (page 176).

EDUCATIONAL STUMBLING BLOCKS

There are two stumbling blocks related to schools embracing Irlen testing. First, schools are philosophically seen in terms of developing skills and knowledge, whether we are talking about basic skills such as reading, writing, and basic math computations or higher level skills such as geometry and science. Anything that is not directly related to skill development is typically not part of a school's direct responsibility. Secondly, if a school recognizes and identifies a problem, that school is then responsible to address the problem or, if necessary, pay for any outside services

Other Issues Not Detected by the Discrepancy Model

It is important to recognize that there are many factors that can contribute to learning disabilities in children that may not be recognized by the standard battery of tests. Here are some areas you may want to consider:

- Allergies (including very common food allergies)
- Eating sensitivities and eating patterns
- Overusing antibiotics to treat infections
- Sensitivity to noise
- Sensitivity to smell
- Sleep patterns and sleep problems
- Thyroid problems

These factors are among the common problems that affect children in a learning environment and are overlooked by testing in the schools. They are also not typically the focus of medical attention. (For more on these factors, see Appendix A on page 176.)

required. While this sounds like a good thing, quite often it tends to backfire. In essence, this law was designed to benefit the parents and the students. However, schools sometimes do not identify issues for fear of having to pay for them.

Regarding Irlen Syndrome, this is particularly exasperating because when a child is identified as having "a general learning issue," it costs far more money to follow the traditional approach than to screen her and provide Irlen Filters. On average, the school spends $10,000 per year for each child who requires special education services, and some children receive these services for years. For some children, a simple screening for Irlen Syndrome would be much more cost-effective.

Teacher by Teacher

It is always advantageous to be able to introduce a new system or methodology to the top and work your way down. In the educational system, that would mean that school superintendents and top administrators would bring a new program into their communities and, from there, into the schools. In our case, it would mean recommending that Irlen screenings be done routinely in order to recognize this specific population of children, which is larger than we had ever initially imagined. Unfortunately, this does not happen very often in the educational system, where outside methodology is very difficult to infuse into a long-standing institution.

Even though I created a screening method that was adaptable and useful for training teachers and psychologists to identify children with Irlen Syndrome, teachers and psychologists continue to be blocked from using these skills by principals and administrators.

Of course the problem was, and remains, that teachers typically have limited power in comparison to the larger system. Nonetheless, thanks to the efforts of individual teachers who managed to get their schools to allow them to do Irlen screenings, children in schools around the country are being screened and given overlays. As a result, these children are showing improvement. Since the late 1980s, nearly 8,000 educators have been trained and millions of children have been given colored overlays, but that is only a drop in the bucket. For every classroom where a child is able to be screened, identified and helped, there are thousands and thousands of classrooms where this is not happening. Remember, the fear is that if the school identifies a problem, it will then be liable to pay for the solution. As a result, the parents of many children never even learn about Irlen Syndrome. In fact, while some schools "get it" and allow teachers to introduce the screening into the schools, others forbid teachers from using this technology, which can be as simple and cost-effective as helping a child by providing a colored overlay.

Dealing with Opposition (or Trying to)

As mentioned earlier, the federal government has, in recent years, been pushing for schools to take more responsibility to identify processing difficulties. This could be very promising, especially for those with Irlen Syndrome, depending on how the schools respond. The hope is that this will allow for such screenings to precede the more expensive IEPs (Individualized Education Plans) and special education needs for this population of students. The concept of using colored overlays to address visual processing deficits has also gained acceptance. In fact, it's very positive that many states now allow colored overlays to be used for standardized testing.

Of course, you would think something that has proven to be helpful in one state would be welcomed in all states, but this is not true. In
Florida, schools cannot identify children as having Irlen Syndrome, and
children are not allowed to use colored overlays. As a result of a ruling
by the Florida Board of Optometry, cease and desist orders were sent to
school districts, and children who were making progress using their colored overlays were forced to stop using them. We have tried for many
years to have this changed. Despite all the research that supports the
position that Irlen Syndrome is a perceptual processing dysfunction, we
have run up against a brick wall. It is sad that children in every other
state in the country and in countries all over the world can use colored
overlays, but children in Florida can't. I wonder why Irlen Filters are considered different than books that have pages in a different color, colored
writing pads, and even colored paper.

FIGHTING THE SYSTEM

Parents do have some power to make changes in the schools, even if
they don't know all the LD "lingo" (see opposite page). In fact, I recall
a case in Alabama in 1991 that set a precedent in favor of children using
Irlen Filters. The case, Robert Robinson versus the Mobile County Board
of School Commissioners, came about after Robert had been screened,
diagnosed, and treated for Irlen Syndrome.[2] Robert then proceeded to
wear his Irlen Filters to school to improve his reading. The principal of
the school, however, decided that Robert could not wear his filters in
school because they would be distracting and a point of contention for
the other students. The principal also decided that teachers did not have
to follow the recommendations made by the Irlen Diagnostician to help
Robert with his reading problems. Both the Irlen Screener from Mobile,
Alabama, and the diagnostician from nearby New Orleans were on
hand at the hearing to give their testimonies. In addition, another Irlen
Screener who had tutored Robert sent written information about having
tutored him.

The settlement of the case contained the following items:

- Information regarding Robert's Irlen Syndrome (at the time still called
  Scotopic Sensitivity Syndrome) would be provided to each of his
  teachers as well as the principal or the principal's designee and the
  school counselor.

- School officials would encourage Robert to use his Irlen Filters.

The "Lingo"

The field of learning disabilities is riddled with acronyms like IEP, SST, RTI, IDEA, NCLB, 504 Plan, and terminology such as "best practices" and "evidence-based methods." Different states, and even school districts within the same states, have their own rules governing the testing and identification for Specific Learning Disabilities (SLD). To delve into an explanation of the various abbreviations is unnecessary for the purpose of this book—I am simply trying to point out that dealing with these issues can be very confusing for parents, or anyone who is not familiar with the "lingo," for that matter.

What does all this mean? It's enough to make your head spin. It is equally confusing for parents, teachers, principals, and administrators. Even educators are having problems understanding and implementing new laws. The saddest part about this process is that it often means the children who need help are not quick to receive it or, in some cases, do not receive help at all.

According to the attorney representing the Robinsons, the outcome of the hearing set a precedent for the state school system to recognize the existence of Irlen Syndrome and to cooperate so that students who needed the filters would be able to use them in the classroom.

One of the factors influencing the decision was that the filters were not unlike prescribed lenses and that children who needed such filters should not be deprived of the right to wear them.

Statistical Realities

The number of children in special education classes continues to increase. In fact, the largest population within the broad disability group is those with learning disabilities. Approximately one in every seven people in the United States has a learning disability. Experts estimate that 10 to 15 percent of the school-aged population in the United States is learning disabled. It is estimated that there are also 6 to 8 million adults with learning disabilities.

A few other statistics that matter:

- Thirty-five percent of children with learning disabilities drop out of high school. This is twice the rate of students without learning disabilities. (Source: National Longitudinal Transition Study)

- Forty-eight percent of people with learning disabilities are out of the workforce or unemployed. (Source: Bridges to Practice)

- Approximately 85 percent of all individuals with learning disabilities have difficulties in the area of reading. (Source: National Institute of Child Health and Human Development)

- Twenty-one million Americans can't read at all, forty-five million are marginally illiterate, and one-fifth of high school graduates can't read their diplomas. (Source: Department of Justice, 1993)

THE TROUBLING TRUTH

While it is easy for me to reflect on some of the many obstacles we have had to overcome, it's eye-opening to review some of the stories that have been sent to me from some of the many Irlen Screeners and supporters. Here are just a few of the stories of their frustration and angst.

The following are abridged versions of some of the letters I received from screeners.

Hi Helen,

This is a personal story. My colleague and I were reading specialists and certified Irlen Screeners. We did not find any difficulty with screening children or having the results implemented in IEPs in our school district.

However, our office secretary's ten-year-old granddaughter, Kathy, was in a neighboring school district and was having great difficulty learning how to read. Kathy's mother asked the school district to test her daughter for Irlen Syndrome. The district refused, saying it was not a legitimate method. So, Kathy's mother and grandmother came to us and asked if we would test Kathy to see if she had Irlen Syndrome. We agreed, tested her, and found that she did indeed have Irlen Syndrome. So, we recommended the use of colored overlays and colored paper. Using the overlays at home provided marked improvement for Kathy, helping her to relax, concentrate on her work, and improve her reading.

However, both Kathy's classroom and LD teachers refused to implement them. An IEP meeting was convened, which we attended as advocates for Kathy. The meeting with the IEP team was cold and hostile. They frequently questioned our credentials, asked why we had tested Kathy, and they didn't like our recommendations in regard to Irlen Syndrome and the overlays.

Finally, due to the insistence of Kathy's mom, the use of overlays and colored paper were added to Kathy's IEP program. These recommendations boosted Kathy's ability to read, and Kathy's classroom teacher acknowledged later on that she was grateful to have had these tools available for Kathy.

However, two days after attending the IEP meeting, my colleague and I were called into the office of our supervisor, the Director of Special Services. She explained that the Director of Special Services in Kathy's school district called her to report us for unprofessional behavior. It is hard to believe that the district was so against using the overlays that they acted in such a vindictive manner, lying and trying to get two IEP advocates—who were also fellow educators— in trouble for helping a student!

—CYNTHIA, IRLEN CLIENT FILES

Dear Helen,

In spite of the large number of children per capita, my state is in the educational dark ages. They practice what I call "education by experimentation," and the students are the ones who suffer. When something is as viable, inexpensive, and backed up with research as Irlen Syndrome is, they turn their noses up at it. I guess that Irlen Syndrome is not complicated enough.

I have fought with the district over the years and have screened many students, primarily those in my classroom. Everyone comments on how calm the kids are in my room and how well they read. The resource teachers over the years often have me screen their really "tough" students and they, too, are believers.

However, getting the Special Ed Department in the district to agree to train the resource teachers to screen for Irlen Syndrome is another matter. Because they have not "really ever heard of this," they believe it couldn't possibly be viable.

—HEIDI, IRLEN CLIENT FILES

Dear Helen,

I was told by the Head of Special Ed for the district and by the school psychologist that I was not allowed to test children for Irlen Syndrome. I was also not allowed to recommend testing to the parents. I was told it was not research-based and that only research-based things were used by the district. They almost made me take out the overlays because every teacher didn't have them to use.

Another reason the district used for not allowing me to test was that there wouldn't be enough people in the district to test everyone, so it wasn't fair for me to test just a few. None of their arguments were logical, but it didn't matter; I was told that I could not test any of the children in my classroom.

Now, I introduce Irlen to students and their parents by having the ones who currently use the lenses or overlays tell their stories at the beginning of the school year. Some kids recognize the symptoms in themselves and tell me they think they have it. I direct them to the Irlen website and tell them to take the online test. It certainly isn't what is supposed to be done, but I don't know any other way to help these kids.

I found when I was testing them, approximately 30 percent of my kids had Irlen Syndrome. Of course, it's great for those who go for the testing, but I know I'm missing many children because I can't do the initial screenings and have the parents see what their kids are going through.

—DENNY, IRLEN CLIENT FILES

These are just a few of the stories from frustrated teachers and screeners. Like many practical and proven solutions that are not supported by district administrators or the Department of Education, the Irlen Method continues to go up against roadblocks.

CONCLUSION

Today there are no surgical procedures, medications, or quick fixes that can eliminate learning problems. However, there are interventions, accommodations, and modifications that can remove some of the barriers, allowing the brain to function better and, thus, allowing children to perform better. These approaches work! Accommodations and interventions may be the keys to opening the doors for the learning disabled population. We must look beyond instruction and repetition as being the only methods for change.

The Irlen Method is one important intervention that allows the brain to function better and thus more accurately process information. It does not eliminate the cause but does remove a barrier. However, the Irlen Method alone cannot solve all of the various learning problems. Parents need to identify the different learning problems and provide a variety of interventions, accommodations, and modifications specifically designed to address their child's specific needs or problems. Parents must have knowledge so that they can provide the power to help their children.

In the next chapter, we will look at some of the positive stories from screeners, parents, and teachers who went the extra mile. We will discuss what you, as a parent, can do to advocate for your child in the schools. Today, it is more important than ever to talk about advocacy. Overcrowded schools, budget cuts, and an ever-increasing emphasis on testing have created school districts that have neither the time nor the funding to look out for your children. Advocacy by parents is necessary across the board, whether it is for Irlen Syndrome, any type of learning disability, or simply to make sure your child is getting the type of specific attention she needs from her school. This holds true for struggling students and those who should be in advanced placement classes. Parents today must be ready to stand up for the needs of their children.

3

Advocacy and Doing the Best for Your Child

> *By the time Jennifer reached the fourth grade, it was obvious that she had a problem. Her grades were dropping, and even though she tested as a bright child with a good vocabulary, her reading and math skills were below average. Neither her teachers nor her parents understood why such a bright child was having difficulty in math, making sloppy errors on her schoolwork, and having trouble copying from the board. She also could not seem to comprehend her reading assignments. The school had no answers. Jennifer was not doing poorly enough to be tested for learning disabilities, yet she was struggling. She never told anyone that she would develop headaches if she read more than a few pages.*
>
> *It was Jennifer's parents who, determined to help their daughter, did the research and found out about Irlen Syndrome. They had her tested to see if this was the possible cause of her problems.*
>
> *Today, Jennifer wears Irlen Filters and the words no longer flash, flicker, or run together without spaces to separate them. Numbers line up in math, and, as a result, she is doing very well in school.*
>
> —JENNIFER, IRLEN CLIENT FILES

It is important to see stories like this one, in which parents make a difference by taking charge and determining what needs to be done for their child. Parents today must advocate for their children, especially when it comes to education and health matters. It is important that as parents, you do not give your power away. You cannot sit back and assume the school is going to be able to either identify the source of a child's difficulties or provide a solution. While schools are designed to educate, they are not in a position to recognize all of the issues that prevent children from learning.

PARENTAL RIGHTS

Before you advocate for your child, you should know your rights as a parent. Federal law states that a school district can use the discrepancy model as a means of identification—but it does not have to and can, instead, use other means of identifying learning disabilities. The law now provides schools with greater discretion in the identification of learning disabilities. Therefore, various states—and sometimes even schools within the same state—will use different methods of identification. As a result, a child receiving services in one state or one school district would not necessarily qualify for the same services in another state or district. Since there is no common way to determine a disability, it is imperative that as parents (and teachers), you have the necessary information to advocate for help.

First, you need to do some research to find out what does and does not qualify your child for identification in your state or school district. This typically means contacting the district office and asking who is in charge of testing children with learning disabilities.

Federal legislation also specifies parents' rights. Parents have a right to participate in the educational decision-making process. Your rights, more specifically, include the following:

- If you disagree with the school regarding test results, placement, services provided, or services not being provided, you may wish to ask for a state mediator or a due process hearing from your state Department of Education. You can also report the school to the U.S. Department of Education for discrimination if you feel (and have some proof) that there has been discrimination practiced against your child.

- Once your child has been identified as having a learning disability and has an IEP (Individualized Education Plan), federal law requires that this label must be recognized by other states and school districts. This means that even if a child moves to another state or school district, the label follows him and appropriate services must be provided. Therefore, when you change districts or move to another state, your child's IEP also follows and he does *not* need to be retested to qualify for services.

- The school must re-evaluate a learning disabled child at least every three years (many do such an evaluation annually).

- You can change your mind and withdraw your child from specific learning disability (SLD) services at any time.

- You may have your child educated in the least restrictive school setting possible. Every effort should be made to develop an educational program that will provide your child with the greatest amount of interaction with children who are not disabled.

- You may obtain an independent evaluation if you disagree with the outcome of the school's evaluation.

- You may participate in the development of your child's IEP. As an important member of the team, you may attend the IEP meeting and share your ideas about your child's special needs, the type of program appropriate for meeting those needs, and the related services the school will provide to help him benefit from his educational program.

- You may request a re-evaluation if you suspect your child's current educational placement is inappropriate.

- You may request an evaluation if you think your child needs special education or related services. Make your request in writing and save a copy for yourself.

- You may review all of your child's records and obtain copies of these records, but the school may charge you a fee for making copies. Only you, as a parent, and those persons directly involved in the education of your child will be given access to his personal records. If you feel any of the information in your child's record is inaccurate, misleading, or violates his privacy or other rights, you may request that the information be changed. If the school refuses your request, you then have the right to request a hearing to challenge the questionable information in your child's records. The school can provide you with the paperwork to request a due process hearing and/or file a complaint with the Office of Civil Rights.

- You must be fully informed by the school of all the rights the law provides you and your child.

- You must be notified whenever the school wishes to evaluate your child, wants to change his educational placement, or refuses your request for an evaluation or a change in placement.

- Your consent in writing is needed for an evaluation and special education placement.

Frustration

When dealing with this type of situation, it is easy to become angry, frustrated, or upset. There is nothing wrong with this. However, it is important to keep trying and never give up.

Some of the common reasons parents typically become angry and frustrated are:

- They assumed that the school would find the problem and come up with an adequate solution.

- They have asked to have their child tested, but the child's school doesn't recognize that there is a problem or that an existing problem is severe enough for testing.

- They have had their child tested but are still not seeing enough progress, even with the school's education plan.

As a parent, these are not satisfactory results. You simply cannot wait for someone to test your child or provide you with answers—especially because sometimes even after testing, there are no noticeable results. As noted in the previous chapter, schools do not often look outside of their primary goal—educating. Therefore, it is up to you to make a difference.

RECOGNIZING THE SIGNS

In addition to Irlen Syndrome, many of the issues discussed throughout the book are hereditary, so some of the signs and symptoms you see in your child you may recognize in yourself. In many cases, we found that parents learned strategies and ways of compensating for their own difficulties. In other cases, parents do not realize that the problem is a perception issue and, instead, attribute their child's symptoms to other factors. One of the best excuses I ever heard came from a young girl who told me that she got headaches because her mom tied her hair in braids that were too tight. However, she still had a headache when she came to see me, and at that point she had not had her hair tied in braids for several years. Clearly, braids could not have been the cause. There are also many people who have become so used to having a specific reaction from an activity, they think it is perfectly normal. For example, someone who falls asleep while reading at night may think that reading is supposed to make you fall asleep. Until we learn otherwise, we become accustomed to the way things are and do not understand how they could—or should—be.

Another issue that results from problems that are not easily recognized is that they are also the impetus for behavioral issues. For example, the frustration of not being able to keep up in school—most often for boys—can lead to a child trying to compensate by becoming a class clown, school bully, or gang member. Angry, frustrated teenagers may also be candidates for drug or alcohol abuse in order to numb the feelings of inferiority from teasing or not being able to keep up with their peers.

These examples are all the more reason why it is important to identify Irlen Syndrome or any other underlying issue while a child is still young. No, it will not solve the overall problem of teen bullying or drug and alcohol abuse, but recognizing the root of a learning difficulty early on may allow a child to gain the confidence he needs to make better choices in life. It also helps him avoid being incorrectly or unfairly labeled by other students or teachers as he goes through school.

This is another reason why, as a parent, you cannot give up when it comes to seeking answers for your child, at any age. Consider the following story from an Irlen Screener:

David is now seventeen years old. His school identified him with behavioral problems but never recognized the reasons behind the problems. He displayed poor behavior, received poor grades, and was unable to focus in class. Even though his parents felt that there might be an underlying reason for his behavioral outbursts, they could not convince the school to test him. He did not study for tests, refused to do homework, and was getting failing grades. His problems became so bad that his parents took him for medical, psychological, and psychiatric evaluations.

When he was fifteen years old, David was diagnosed with depression, hospitalized, and then placed on medication. His mother disagreed with the diagnosis that he was depressed. "He seems like a nice kid at home and does not seem to have the same problems," was her response. After years of constantly seeking help from medical, psychological and educational professionals, David's parents did not know where to turn. Nonetheless, they never stopped requesting testing.

Finally, at sixteen David was tested for learning disabilities—but did not qualify. By that time, he had been suspended from school numerous times for fighting and noncompliance. His parents decided to withdraw him from school and tried home teaching. Even then, they never gave up or stopped searching for an answer.

After years of unsuccessful searches and failed attempts, David's parents came across information about the Irlen Method on the internet. David's life, and the life of his parents, has since changed.

—DAVID, IRLEN CLIENT FILES

In David's case, the issue was Irlen Syndrome. For other children, it may be dietary concerns or any number of factors that were never addressed. The point of David's story is that parents should never give up.

You Know Your Child Best

Parents, I first want you to keep in mind that you know your child better than anyone else does. Therefore, you must trust your instincts and your judgment when it comes to making decisions for your child. As a parent, you have the knowledge and information at your fingertips, so never buy into the idea that the school or anyone else has some special knowledge about your child that you do not have.

This goes for labels as well. If your child is labeled as depressed or having ADD, ADHD or anything else, you need to take a realistic look at him and decide whether or not you agree with the diagnosis. If you do, then see if the resulting medication or treatment helps. If you do not agree, your child may have been misdiagnosed. In this case, you should continue looking for the root of the problem. If you simply do not see your child as depressed, or he only appears to be depressed in certain environments, you may be looking at something other than depression. Be a detective and try to find the cause of your child's behavior.

Consider the following story of parents who worked hard to assess their daughter's problem and provide the necessary help. They kept on trying and finally found the answer.

When my daughter was in first grade, she would beg not to go to school any more. She would say she could not do what the other kids did. I'd say, "Of course you can." I asked the school to have her tested for learning issues because I have learning issues. They tested her and found nothing.

In second grade, her teacher told me that she was not doing much work in class, and that when she did do her work, she was never getting it finished. I also noticed that she was not reading as well as her friends were. I asked her physician if she had ADHD, and we tried medication. It didn't help.

In the first month of third grade, the teacher called and said, "Something is going on here. I don't know what, but if we don't figure it out soon, I'm going to lose her." So this time, both the teacher and I asked the school to test her again, and again they found nothing, no learning problems and average-to-high-average intelligence!

I knew she was very bright, but what could I do? Her reading was labored and choppy and without fluency. She hated to read and avoided it at all costs. She often complained that she got headaches and stomachaches while reading, and she said that things on the page moved. I thought there was something wrong with her.

I took her to her doctor, but she was fine. So I took her to the eye doctor, and again she was fine. After that, she would cry and say, "No one understands me!" One night, while my husband was tucking her into bed, he asked her, "What do you think it is?" She replied, "I think I am allergic to numbers and letters." We had to laugh to ourselves.

One person suggested that she might be light sensitive. I replied, "Are you kidding? Not my daughter; she is on the beach all summer and almost never wears sunglasses while in the sun all day." Finally, someone from the school suggested testing her for something called Irlen Syndrome. I told them to go for it.

That night I found a quiet spot and started to read Helen Irlen's book Reading by the Colors. *My mouth hung open and I said to myself, "Oh my God." I was reading about myself and my daughter! Sure enough, the test confirmed that she had Irlen Syndrome. We had finally found the answer!*

—JOANNE, IRLEN CLIENT FILES

Again, this is a story of diligence on the part of parents who refused to let their daughter struggle. By playing detectives, they were able to find a solution. Obviously, Irlen will not always be the answer, but it is easy to test for, so it is something to be considered when reading troubles, behavior and attention problems, and learning difficulties are thought to be the problem.

The Signs of Irlen Syndrome

If you suspect that your child might have Irlen Syndrome, you will want to look for signs. Remember, your child can be diagnosed as learning disabled, ADD, ADHD, as a gifted child, or none of the above and still have processing problems. With that in mind, the following list provides some of the many signs associated with Irlen Syndrome. You may find that your son or daughter has a couple of these or several of them. Don't panic! Remember, testing is very simple.

■ Initial Signs of Irlen Syndrome

- Common complaints while reading, doing homework, or working at the computer:

    Eye strain or fatigue

    Feeling tired or sleepy

    Frequent headaches

    Words (and/or letters and numbers) getting blurry or hard to see

- Common problems while doing mathematics:

    Has trouble lining up numbers in columns or rows

    Has trouble with forms and shapes in geometry

    Has trouble with word problems

    Makes sloppy, careless errors

    Misreads symbols

- Reading-related behaviors:

    Complains that words or letters do not stay still on page

    Constantly avoids reading

    Falls asleep from reading

    Has trouble tracking (being able to smoothly follow across a line of print or from the end of one line to the beginning of the next line)

    Misreads words

    Needs to re-read for comprehension

    Reads in dim lighting

    Reads slowly or with hesitation

    Skips words or lines when reading

    Takes frequent breaks or gets easily distracted

- Writing characteristics:

    Has difficulty copying from a book or the board

    Has difficulty staying on the line

    Is slow and cannot keep up when copying

    Makes errors while copying

    Unequal letter size

    Unequal spacing

    Writes on a slope, up- or downhill

These and other signs (which you can find at www.irlen.com) are among those that you, as a parent, should be looking out for. However, there is more to it. You must also consider three very important factors: consistency, strategy, and time.

Consistency

It is a good idea to look for patterns in the way your child approaches reading and how soon after beginning reading he wants to stop. In some cases, students and young children will know that after ten or fifteen minutes, their eyes or head will start to hurt, and if they continue, they will get headaches or the words will become hard to see. This is their "trigger point" where the symptoms of Irlen Syndrome start setting in. They have become so familiar with their limits that they will start looking up or away from the page, need a snack, want to take a break, or find some reason to stop reading. Again, if this is a consistent pattern, consider it a red flag that something isn't right.

Strategy

Another way of finding out if your child is struggling is to look at whether or not he is using strategies to cover up a problem. Many children and adults use strategies as ways of compensating or getting around a problem. This may mean trying to play music without reading the notes, doing math problems by head instead of on paper, or trying to remember what was said in class rather than doing the reading or studying for tests. Clearly, strategies are not only used by students with Irlen Syndrome—students with other types of processing or learning problems may use strategies as well. For example, many students use shortcuts while doing their work. The question is whether or not the student using strategies could do the work without them. There is a difference between taking a shortcut to save time and using shortcuts as a crutch. If the student cannot do the work without the strategies, this should also be a red flag that there may be a problem. (The quiz on the opposite page will help you determine if your child is using strategies.)

Strategies are a way of compensating for skills that are either difficult to master or have not yet been developed. People used to think that strategies would prevent a skill from developing, but this is no longer true. Babies are taught to do baby signs before they can talk as a way of being able to express themselves. This does not delay language from developing. As a matter of fact, when the child is able to talk, he generally stops signing. Clearly, strategies can be useful; but when a child continues to use a strategy rather than moving on to the next level, it can signal that there is a problem.

What typically happens to students who depend on strategies to find their way around a problem like Irlen Syndrome is at some point the work will get harder and the student will "hit the wall," being unable to succeed further using the strategies he had been depending on. For example, one commonly used strategy by those with Irlen Syndrome is what I call "skip reading." This is where the individual reads the beginning and end of the textbook chapters rather than all of the assigned material. While this may be okay if you are reading for pleasure, it does not bode well for school exams, where teachers are often looking for specific facts embedded in the core of the material. Equally problematic are those who try to succeed in school without reading at all. Students who manage to succeed doing this in middle and high school will usually realize that it does not work in college or graduate school.

The quiz on the next page contains questions that will help you assess whether or not your child is using compensatory strategies. The idea here is not to question whether such activities have been used once or twice, but whether the strategy is being utilized frequently. Answering "yes" to any of the questions indicates that compensatory strategies are being used.

Time

Children with Irlen Syndrome may not have any problems when they first start to read. As the child continues to read, however, his reading may deteriorate. You may start to notice some of the common symptoms (see list starting on page 48). Do not expect your child to report a problem. You will most likely need to ask.

Compensatory Strategies Quiz

This quiz can help you determine whether or not your child is using strategies at school and at home to minimize strain while reading and completeing assignments.

Circle the answer that best describes your child's situation.

1. Does your child find it impossible to finish reading an entire book?   Yes   No

2. Do you need to summarize books for your child?   Yes   No

3. Does your son or daughter use CliffsNotes/SparkNotes or similar shorter versions of books?   Yes   No

4. Does your child avoid textbook reading?   Yes   No

5. Does your child read beginnings or endings of paragraphs or chapters rather than the entire thing?   Yes   No

6. Has your child passed courses by listening in class without doing assigned reading?   Yes   No

7. Does your son or daughter work hard to get good grades but seems to be smarter than the grades indicate?   Yes   No

The answers to some of these questions may not be forthcoming, as your child may not want to admit to using, or even be aware that he is using such strategies. Therefore, you need to be a detective. For example, look for an unopened textbook three months into the school year or check for other signs that your child avoids reading, such as asking for explanations that could clearly have been found in the reading assignments or constantly missing written instructions that should be read doing other types of activities.

I sometimes ask students to tell me what it feels like after they have been reading for awhile. When the response is, "My head hurts," parents often react in amazement and disbelief. They generally say, "You never told me that!" To which the child typically responds, "You never asked." It's all about communication. Ask your child what he is experiencing. Ask if this is a one-time occurrence or if these headaches occur on a regular basis when reading, doing homework, or by the end of the school day.

If you ask your child about symptoms during the first several minutes he is reading and you get a "no" response, it doesn't mean that after ten, fifteen, or even thirty minutes he won't be struggling. Make sure to have your child try reading for some time and watch to see if any of the problems on the list (see page 48) appear after fifteen, twenty, or thirty minutes. If the child says "no" early on, too many parents immediately come to the conclusion that everything is fine when, in reality, it may simply be that a short time later everything is not fine. If your child tells you there is no problem, let some time pass and then ask again. For those with Irlen Syndrome, reading always gets more difficult as duration increases because the brain has to work harder and harder to process the information.

Standardized tests impose time constraints on the student's ability to perform. Many times, a child with Irlen Syndrome will know the material and still do poorly on a test. For the most part, the only thing that is considered is the total score of right and wrong answers. Therefore, if a child is asked twenty questions on a half-hour exam, and gets twelve right (60 percent), it is assumed that he did not understand the work, did not study hard enough, or just is unable to do the work. However, what may be missed is that he got nine of the first ten questions correct and only three of the second ten questions correct. What may be happening is that Irlen Syndrome is kicking in after ten or fifteen minutes, and the child is struggling on the second half of the exam, going from a very successful 90 percent to a very poor 30 percent. The total number of right and wrong answers is, therefore, not fully representative of how he did on the exam, nor does it show that the ability to perform deteriorated as the student progressed. While you cannot make such a judgment from only one test, if the pattern continues, it would be a red flag that there is a problem because performance gets worse over time.

APPROACHING YOUR CHILD

Nobody wants to think of their child as anything less than perfect. The truth, however, is that no one is perfect, and the best thing you can do for your child is help make his life better by solving as many problems as you can. Later on, as he gets older, you will guide him in how to solve problems for himself.

When approaching your child, it is very important to let him know that there is no right or wrong answer and nothing he says will make you angry. Wanting to please you, children may give you the answers they think you want to hear. Younger children (and sometimes older ones) may be concerned that you will be upset with their answers or that you will be disappointed in them. Children sometimes have a tendency to feel ashamed because they know they are not doing as well as you would like them to do in school. In some cases, they are ashamed that they are using strategies to succeed and feel that this is cheating.

You need to be reassuring, while also letting your child know that everyone does things in different ways. What often helps in such situations is breaking the ice by sharing your own personal stories of how you struggled and had to compensate. After all, Irlen Syndrome is hereditary, so your child may be experiencing the same things that you experienced and is compensating in a similar manner. However, even if your experiences differed from those of your child, as can be the case, the idea of sharing your own struggles can still show your imperfections and get the ball rolling when it comes to opening up the lines of communication. Even if your personal struggles are not reading-related, you should still share them. By opening up and sharing, problems no longer seem as secretive. Plus, you are showing some vulnerability, which will likely make your child less insecure about showing his.

I remember one parent who told me how she managed to get through school by taking classes with her cousin who enjoyed reading and would read to her. When she got married, she never told her husband that she couldn't read. Instead, she told him that she didn't have time to read. He would read her college books to her while she cooked dinner and did the dishes. She didn't want anyone to know that she had struggled in school. When her daughter started having the same problems, she got nervous. However, her nerves quickly turned to anger when her daughter's school wasn't able to help. She continued to keep her own issues a secret until she came in with her daughter to be tested for Irlen Syndrome. When she realized that there was a reason for her inability to read and that there was nothing to be ashamed of, she gladly shared her struggles with her daughter.

The following note came from one of our Australian screeners who wanted to share the importance of talking with and advocating for your child.

I find that most parents have never asked their children what they see. They, like the teachers, take it for granted. Children can't tell you that what they see is different than what you or I might see because they have always seen print a certain way. They don't realize that there is another way . . . they have no frame of reference. Many times, questionnaires completed by parents without their child's input are incorrect. The greatest difficulty is getting the parents to be willing to admit that their child has a problem.

Maybe the way to go is to have a parent support group, where parents can exchange information on what works when it comes to helping their children. At least then they would have a lobby group for achieving equal opportunity for their children.

—ALICIA, IRLEN CLIENT FILES

Unfortunately, there are not many parent support groups, although being active in your district's parent-teacher association (PTA) can sometimes be beneficial. In an age of two-income families with very busy parents trying to manage jobs and raise families simultaneously, making time for such groups can be difficult. Nonetheless, you can make an effort to communicate with other parents and share ideas on helping your children within the school system, whatever the concerns may be.

From eating vegetables, to going to the dentist, to going for an Irlen screening, it's all about how you approach and present an issue to a child. If, for example, you seem worried, apprehensive, or cynical about the possible response, then your child will pick up on your concern. Children have a very strong innate ability to respond to your moods and feelings. However, they may not understand the nature of your concern. As a parent, you may be hoping that Irlen Syndrome is the cause of your child's struggles because, as you will see in the next chapter, there is a simple solution: Irlen Spectral Filters. But you may also have some trepidation. What if it is something else? What if your child doesn't have Irlen Syndrome? What if your child won't wear the filters? We hear these same concerns from many parents. As an old commercial used to say, the trick is to "never let them see you sweat." In other words, as a parent, you need to be confident and start by taking the preliminary step—getting your child screened.

CONCLUSION

In this chapter, we focused on the need for parents to get involved and advocate, as necessary, for their children when it comes to education and health matters, both of which apply in the case of Irlen Syndrome. Not only do parents need to look for signs as to why their child is not doing well in school, but they also need to learn what the school is offering in the way of help and what is actually working. For various reasons, including poor funding and overcrowded schools, many children are not getting the attention they need. As a result, parents need to be vigilant.

To make matters worse, Irlen Syndrome is not well-known to the majority of teachers and school psychologists, and more "fashionable" labels may be placed on a child who exhibits certain academic difficulties or behaviors. In upcoming chapters, we will look further at other issues with symptoms that may be confused with Irlen Syndrome.

Most significantly, in this chapter we stressed the importance of being aware of how your child acts and behaves in various situations and not always listening to other people's assessments. Remember, first and foremost, that you know your child best.

In the next chapter, we will look at the Irlen Method and go into detail on what it means to have your child tested.

4

Irlen Testing:
What It's All About

Dear Helen,

I'm certain you have received countless letters like this one, which nearly stopped me from writing one of my own. But, I just can't hold back the joy I am feeling. It is 7:53 AM on a Friday morning, just three days after I was screened by you for Irlen Syndrome. I left your office following the screening with two different overlays.

For the first time in my life, I am able to read for more than a half hour without stopping or developing a headache.

The rose-colored overlay seemed to work the best for me. It allowed me to experience the feeling of reading with an effortless flow for the first time in my life. I have never been able to stream information into my head from the printed page the way I can from audio or video tapes. Now I can! My only problem now is that I need a new book to read!

I can't thank you and your staff enough for all the great work that you are doing!

Warmest regards,
DEREK

Thank you, Derek, for the above note. Before moving on to the many causes of Irlen and Irlen-like symptoms, it is important to take a look at the screening process. It is a painless and uncomplicated process that can first effectively determine if you and/or your child have Irlen Syndrome, and, secondly, if you do, find the right color—or color combination—that can correct all of the symptoms associated with Irlen Syndrome.

IRLEN SCREENING

The first stage of the Irlen Method is called a screening. During this testing session, people with Irlen Syndrome can be identified and the severity of the issue can be determined. Screening is a diagnostic tool and a means of educating the client and family members about their unique set of symptoms. There are three parts to the testing session.

- Part one determines if an individual has the type of perpetual processing problems that are associated with Irlen Syndrome.

- Part two uses a variety of perceptual tasks which, for those with Irlen Syndrome, elicit the same distortions and physical symptoms that occur when reading. This creates an awareness of each individual's unique array of symptoms and makes it easier to describe each of the symptoms.

- For those with Irlen Syndrome, part three eliminates the perceptual distortions and physical symptoms by determining the correct overlay color, or combination of colors, specifically for each individual.

The final step is determining the amount of improvement in reading rate, fluency, comprehension, and comfort using the correct color. Education is an important part of the screening process. During the screening, simple perceptual tasks are used to elicit information about the type (or types) of distortions and physical symptoms that occur at some point while reading or performing other academic tasks. The screening creates awareness of symptoms, using language to describe the problems, and educating the individual about what a page of words, numbers, or music is supposed to look like. Screening also explains what it is they are seeing that is causing a problem. Something we say a lot because it is worth repeating is that no one knows what reading is like for anyone else. No one can see through the eyes of someone else, nor can anyone know how another person's brain processes information.

Additionally, the screening process aims to identify other family members who might be struggling with Irlen Syndrome. You may be wondering why this is important. Often, only the child who is failing in school is identified with a problem and tested. Children who are doing well academically are often overlooked. The screening method teaches parents how to identify Irlen Syndrome. At the end of the testing session, it is not unusual for parents to realize that they have been ignoring the sibling who is doing well in school but doesn't enjoy reading; the sibling who gets good grades but spends extra hours doing homework; the child who does not appear to be reaching her potential; or the child who complains of headaches, stomachaches, or tiredness when reading. As mentioned, parents often realize during the screening process that they have been suffering from Irlen Syndrome themselves.

Since Irlen Syndrome is complex and occurs on a continuum from slight to severe, the screening process also provides information on the severity of the problem. Usually, the parent who accompanies the child is not only sitting in during the testing to observe the entire process, but also gets to participate by doing some of the tasks and finding out if they, too, are a candidate. It can be an eye-opener for the parent who suddenly discovers why reading was so difficult when she was in school. The screening process allows the parent to put the pieces of the puzzle together for herself as well as for her child. It also provides answers so that the child no longer feels at fault for not succeeding.

Finally, those who are diagnosed with Irlen Syndrome do not leave the screening empty-handed. Once the optimal colored overlay—or combination of overlays—is determined, the individual gets to take the overlay(s) home. The color or color combination is verified by doing a variety of tasks that include measuring reading rate, fluency, and error rate. The color should make an immediate difference—not just in the testing situation, but also when used at home. The parent is surprised and thrilled with the improvement during testing. Everyone leaves with their own overlay to use at home, at school, and on the computer. This allows everyone to try using the overlays in a variety of situations to make sure that they see improvement, even when reading for longer periods.

However, not everyone who is screened has Irlen Syndrome and leaves with an overlay. Often there are other reasons for reading difficulties or other problems that coexist and need to be addressed. In these cases, suggestions and recommendations are given to the parents regarding other methods that should be pursued.

In some cases, reading problems continue for some students even after they receive their overlay, because certain reading skills still need to be developed with instruction and remediation.

Alleviating Fears

The screening process has been carefully designed to enhance comfort and alleviate the fears of both parents and children. This is extremely important because we do not want anyone to feel alone, singled out, or afraid.

We see a lot of fear about being tested, especially from adults. This is very understandable because by the time they are thinking about being screened by us, they have usually tried so many things and nothing has worked. They don't want to set themselves up for hope and another failure. As a result, they are typically more apprehensive than children are prior to the screening process. For many, it is very hard to believe that there is actually a viable solution out there after years trying many different things that did not make a difference.

Many times, adults fear acknowledging a problem, even though they know there is something wrong. This is not at all unusual. It's similar to not wanting to go to the doctor when you are sick because you fear the doctor will only confirm your belief. The thinking is that if you ignore the symptoms, you won't have to deal with the problem. Unfortunately, such thinking usually only makes things worse. For example, many people avoid going to the dentist with a toothache because they hate the experience. In time, however, the pain caused by the toothache gets so bad that it simply cannot be avoided. People tend to put things off, and, unfortunately, an Irlen Screening—which is certainly far less painful than having a tooth filled—seems to fall into that category.

I'm still amazed by the parents who have known about the Irlen Method for years and have waited to bring their children in for screening. By that time, these children have experienced years of frustration and are now feeling bad about themselves. The reality is that many people wait, hoping everything will get better. Unfortunately, that is not the case with Irlen Syndrome—it does not just go away.

Who Can Screen?

Both Irlen Screeners and Irlen Diagnosticians can administer the screening tests. We get a lot of calls at the Irlen Institute checking to make sure our screeners are certified, and I must say that we welcome such calls. Irlen Screeners and Diagnosticians *must* be certified, and it is important that before you have either your child or yourself screened, you have confidence that the professional has been properly trained. Additionally, you shouldn't try to self-screen (see opposite page).

Those who screen go through a formal training process. Training lasts for two days, and then trainees go out and practice testing. After completing the training, they become certified. Since information in this area changes (and increases with research and clinical practice), we require that those who screen must attend classes in order to be re-certified every five years.

At present, there are thousands of screeners in the United States alone, with many others in Asia, Australia, South and Central America, New Zealand, Africa, Canada, and throughout Europe. However, not everyone can be trained as an Irlen Screener. Irlen Screeners include teachers and university professors, heads of learning assistance centers at major universities, psychologists, neuropsychologists, therapists (including those for speech and language), occupational therapists, a few optometrists, ophthalmologists, and even some chiropractors. Their backgrounds are quite diverse; but for the most part, they are predominantly highly-skilled professionals in a wide variety of fields who have an understanding of, and are familiar with, individuals who have learning and reading difficulties.

While some screeners are listed on the Irlen Institute's website (www.irlen.com), it is easier to find a screener through one of the Irlen Diagnosticians, who are located all around the United States and throughout the world. Certified Diagnosticians, who undergo a more rigorous and intensive training and certification process than screeners, also maintain lists of currently active screeners in the outlying area. Irlen

---

Self-Screening Is Not Effective

It is important to point out that self-screening is not effective. Therefore, I strongly suggest that you do not try to do the screening yourself. The major concern is that because you and/or your child are unaware of what the page is *supposed* to look like, you have no way of knowing whether or not you are truly making things better. What is worse is that if you select the wrong color, you may think that color in general does not work, which is, of course, not the case with the right colored overlays.

Screening by a trained Irlen Screener or Diagnostician can not only lead to the right colored overlay(s) (which sometimes means utilizing a combination of as many as four or five colors), but it can provide knowledge, information, and awareness about the actual problem as well as answers to any questions you may have. While it typically won't hurt to play around with colors at home, it is far more beneficial to have an Irlen certified professional who is trained and knowledgeable do the test and provide the best color. This is the only way to get optimal results. I might also add that in some instances, selecting the wrong color can cause physical symptoms such as discomfort and stress—so be careful.

Diagnosticians are responsible for staying in touch with screeners and making sure they remain up-to-date on the latest findings and research. In addition, the Irlen Institute holds conferences on a regular basis in order to update basic skills and introduce new information.

IRLEN SPECTRAL FILTERS

Screening will identify if you have Irlen Syndrome and, if you do, allow you to experience the immediate difference color can make for reading, which is typically considered to be the major issue. But when you think of reading, you need to expand your definition. You don't just read print from the page of a book; you read information from a whiteboard, from a computer screen, and as you write or copy material. Even while doing math problems, you are looking at the numbers on a page, which is also a perceptual activity. There are a lot of perceptual activities that are involved in learning. In fact, I don't think there is anything that you do in school that does not involve perception.

If you recall from Chapter 1, it was the students from the initial study at California State University in Long Beach who came to me, thanked me for helping them with reading, and then asked for more help. They explained that the issue expanded further than just reading from a textbook. From their initial concern came years of research and testing that culminated in the Irlen Filters used today.

It is these filters, which are in the form of lenses (glasses or contacts), that are the next step in the process. The overlays that were previously discussed are a diagnostic tool intended to provide a sense of the benefits Irlen Spectral Filters can provide. The use of an overlay changes the color contrast so that the reader is seeing a blue page or a green page. It is a way of showing each individual with Irlen Syndrome how color can be a great help. Irlen Spectral Filters, on the other hand, do so much more than the overlays.

The process may appear to be rather simple but is actually quite complex. Diagnosticians have a lens kit that consists of every color in the spectrum of visible light. This enables them to create color combinations that are different for every individual. Everyone's brain is different, so everyone needs their own unique combination of colors in their lenses. The diagnostician establishes the part of the light spectrum that needs to be filtered and the degree to which it needs to be filtered. Once the individual's unique color is determined, the individual goes through a variety of activities—including reading, looking at a computer screen, going outside, and so on. The right combination will enable the individual to notice improvements with not only reading, but also all areas that require visual perception including motor skills, depth perception, sports performance, and even driving at night.

Filters Are *NOT* Colored Glasses

One of the common misconceptions, and perhaps a major reason why some people are hesitant to explore the possibility of Irlen Spectral Filters, is the belief that pink or blue tinted lenses will cause them to see the world in pink or blue. That is not the case at all. Irlen Filters do not change the color of someone's world. When looking through pink, blue, rose, or any other Irlen Filter, the wearer still sees the world as it appears. The white page will still appear white—unlike the colored overlays, which do make the printed page appear a different color. The lenses are carefully designed to filter only the color, or colors, in the visible light spectrum that are causing the perceptual problem for the individual.

Another misconception is that wearing dark glasses is necessary to make the environment less bright and more comfortable. This is not true. Often, people will try to help themselves by putting on sunglasses and making everything darker. However, sunglasses—while reducing some brightness and glare—also filter all of the light frequencies across the entire light spectrum. So, as a result, they make everything darker. Therefore, you cannot wear sunglasses to make it less bright and more comfortable when reading or sitting in a classroom with fluorescent lighting. In addition, you cannot see much of anything at night if you try to wear your sunglasses while driving to block out the brightness from headlights and street lights. With Irlen Spectral Filters, which are unlike sunglasses, things stay bright but remain comfortable, which is a completely new feeling to someone with Irlen Syndrome. Because of this, people can wear Irlen Filters all the time and still be able to see clearly. Again, only the specific colors or wavelengths of light that are causing the brain to have difficulty processing visual information are being filtered, which is why color selection should be done only by a certified Irlen Diagnostician.

Annual Filter Checks

While many types of therapies used to treat illnesses or recover from injuries can take several months and a number of return visits, treatment for Irlen Syndrome does not fall into that category. You will not need weekly or even monthly visits in order to see a difference. Once you have your Irlen Spectral Filters, you will see an immediate change. In fact, you typically will not return until you come back for an annual filter check. Yearly re-evaluations of your Irlen Filters by a certified Irlen Diagnostician are essential. As with all colors, including those on fabric, in paint, on printed pages, etc., light can cause colors to fade or even morph slightly into a different shade. Because the change is gradual, you may not even realize that this is happening. The result is that even with slight changes, the filters lose their benefit. Do not panic if this happens! A slight modification by a certified Irlen Diagnostician can be made and result in the lenses being just as effective as they were at the start.

> *Shelly, a school psychologist, has been wearing her Irlen Filters for almost twenty years. Every year, she comes in for her filter check even though her color has never changed.*
>
> *On the other hand, Sue started wearing Irlen Filters in third grade; and as she has grown, her color has changed. Her mother has gotten very good at being able to identify when Sue's filters are not working and immediately brings her in for a filter check.*
>
> *Reid started wearing Irlen Filters in fourth grade. In sixth grade, he grew at least six inches. Not only did his clothes not fit, but his Irlen Filters were not working as well. He was noticing that he couldn't read as long as he used to, was getting tired while reading, and started re-reading pages for comprehension. Along with needing larger clothes, he needed his lens color changed. With his new color, everything was as good as it had been for the past few years.*
>
> —IRLEN CLIENT FILES

If your Irlen Filters aren't helping like they did when you first started wearing them, do not feel that the technology has stopped working for you. There are plenty of people around the world who have been wearing Irlen Filters for twenty years or longer, dating back to when we first provided those in the original study with colored glasses. Remember, once color works for you, color in general should continue to work for you—even if the color itself changes over time.

There are a few different things that can cause Irlen Filters to become less effective or stop working entirely, such as:

• Accidents, especially traumatic head injuries, whiplash, or blows to the head

- Anesthesia associated with a medical operation or oral dental surgery

- Changes in a visual prescription

- Chemotherapy

- Emotional trauma or significant stress, such as death or divorce

- Gradual fading of the original color

- Growth spurts or hormonal changes (including puberty)

- Illness (including high fevers)

- Some antibiotics, medications, or drugs including *Viagra*, steroids, ventilators, medication for asthma, and birth control pills

While in many cases no changes take place, the items on the list are all possibilities and reasons why you should go to have your lenses checked annually. However, in some cases, you may need to get checked more than once a year. (See inset below.)

While Irlen Spectral Filters will be effective as soon as an individual puts them on—without any practice or training involved—they should not be perceived as a magical end-all to academic problems. Changing the ability to be able to perform does not necessarily eliminate bad study

---

Key Indicators That It Is Time for a Filter Check

If you notice any of the symptoms on the following list in either yourself or your child, it is time to head back to an Irlen Diagnostician for a filter check.

- A change in coordination and/or depth perception occurs. For example, you or your child start tripping, bumping into things, having problems driving or judging distances, or dropping things more often than usual.

- The length of time you or your child can read comfortably for has decreased since you first received your Irlen Filters.

- Reading has become difficult or uncomfortable again.

- Symptoms such as headaches, stomachaches, dizziness, nausea, fatigue, eye strain, restlessness, fidgeting, irritability, or anxiety start occurring more frequently.

- You find yourself or your child being combative and argumentative.

habits or change personal motivation, self-concept, attitude toward school, or academic performance. Academic improvement may not occur immediately, as the student may need to develop new skills through instruction, learn new habits, break old habits, and learn to trust the process. Remember, while Irlen Filters can make the page clear, stable, and comfortable, it is still up to the student to take the time to open and read the book, practice reading, or learn basic reading skills.

OTHER OPTIONS

Obviously, the best manner of taking care of Irlen Syndrome is to have a screening and subsequently wear your Irlen Filters, either as contacts or as glasses.

If, however, you have not yet seen an Irlen Diagnostician you and/or your child can utilize some other strategies. The following are some of the many options that may be helpful.

Using Colored Paper for Assignments

Children with Irlen Syndrome should avoid white paper and use recycled or colored paper for assignments, reports, or writing whenever possible. When using white paper, there may be insufficient contrast between the letters and the background. The white may dominate, causing strain, fatigue, and perceptual distortions. Also, experiment with different ink colors to see which is most compatible and readable on the colored paper chosen.

Using Colored Paper for Tests and Handouts

Due to the distortions and discomfort caused by white paper, tests and hand-outs should be xeroxed onto the child's preferred color of paper. Discuss this with the child's teachers to make sure this is acceptable. Explain why this is necessary for the child.

Avoiding Bright Lights

Fluorescent lighting and bright lighting (often in schools) can cause strain, loss of concentration, and perceptual distortions. Someone experiencing these symptoms should sit near a window and use indirect natural lighting or dim lighting whenever possible to read and work. If there is enough natural light coming into the room, ask if the row of fluorescent lights under which your child is sitting can be turned off.

Wearing a Brimmed Hat or Visor

To reduce strain and fatigue, an individual with Irlen Syndrome can wear a brimmed hat or visor in heavily lit areas (like classrooms) as well as in other places, such as supermarkets and shopping malls. The underside of the brim should be a dark color, such as blue, green, or black. If the sufferer in question is your child, you will likely need to discuss such an accommodation with the school since hats are usually not allowed inside the classroom.

Using a Magnifying Bar or Sheet

A magnifying bar or magnifying sheet can improve reading rate and comprehension by increasing spacing, definition, and span of recognition. The magnifier can also be used for mathematics, diagrams, charts, maps, dictionaries, and copying in order to increase speed and accuracy.

Using a Bookstand

For some individuals, the position of reading material can affect the ease of reading. The material to be read or copied should be placed on an angle in order to reduce glare. An adjustable bookstand or book holder can prove helpful.

Using Colored Book Markers

Use of a colored book marker (above or below the line being read) can be helpful in improving accuracy and speed. Some individuals become more efficient readers by using markers to highlight or underline words; others by using a marker on top of the line; others by using the marker after the word being read to block off the rest of the sentence. The color of the marker should not be white, but black or preferably the same as the colored overlay (if the individual has one).

Avoiding Standard Test Answer Sheets

Individuals with Irlen Syndrome sometimes receive poor grades due to errors on tests. These errors are not due to a lack of knowledge, but rather an inability to track and mark the correct spot on the answer sheet, especially on Scantron or fill-in answer sheets. Using a ruler or colored marker may help with tracking. If this is not helpful, the student may need to record the answers on the test itself and allow someone else to transfer the answers onto the answer sheet. Again, you'll need to discuss this with the child's teacher or school in advance.

Additional suggestions and accommodations are provided in Appendix B (see page 184).

CONCLUSION

In this chapter, we walked you through the process of being tested. It is a non-invasive process that can help determine whether you or your child has Irlen Syndrome and whether the Irlen Filters (either glasses or contacts) will be beneficial. Adults accompany their children through the process, easing their fears and often benefiting—for many times, they too discover that they have Irlen Syndrome. Remember, it's hereditary.

Once someone is wearing Irlen Filters, there is a need to get annual filter checks to make sure the color has not faded or that the color needed has not changed. In addition, we provided some other options for those individuals who have not yet been tested but are struggling in the classroom or workplace.

In the next chapter, we take a closer look at the manner in which reading is affected by Irlen Syndrome and what can be done to make reading easier.

5

Reading and Irlen Syndrome

> *"Tim, it's your turn to read."*
> *He sat staring at the bright white page*
> *which had blurry black letters and curvy rivers.*
> *They made him fidget and gave him the shivers.*
> *"Please, I think I need some Magic Glasses*
> *to help me read."*
>
> —FROM "MAGIC GLASSES" BY CAROL STACY

The majority of children and adults who come for Irlen testing have reading difficulties and are hoping for a solution. Many have spent thousands of dollars on remediation, educational therapists, tutors, and other therapies. Some have received services from their schools in the form of Reading Recovery, Title 1, or RSP. Others are adults who gave up hope long ago.

Because reading problems are complex and can be caused by a wide variety of factors, not everyone who comes for Irlen testing will be identified as having Irlen Syndrome. In this chapter, I will discuss the various types of struggling readers whose problems *can* be helped and improved by the Irlen Method.

THE MYSTERY OF THE STRUGGLING READER

There are nearly 7 million special education students in the United States, and roughly half of them have learning disabilities. A majority of those disabilities are reading-related, such as dyslexia or problems with processing information. Such disabilities are not only found among grade-schoolers who are learning to read, but are more common than you may think in older children and adults as well.

All of this begs the question of why there so many struggling readers. Reading difficulties can be a mystery. Like learning disabilities, reading difficulties are not a distinct disorder—there are numerous variations. Presently, tests do not discriminate between the types of reading difficulties, nor do they tell us the cause of whichever difficulty we may be suffering from.

Therefore, all types of reading problems are handled with instruction, practice, and repetition. As a result, experts continue to debate what reading is, how people learn to do it, and what might be considered the most effective method of teaching reading skills. What is fascinating, however, is that while there is an ongoing debate regarding the best way to teach reading, some children enter kindergarten already knowing how to read and many learn to read regardless of how they are taught. One may wonder how this is possible. The answer is that we may need to look further than classroom teaching methods to understand and address reading problems.

For our purposes, we will stay out of the debate over reading methods. The Irlen Method does not teach a child how to read; rather, it removes perceptual roadblocks that can hold back progress. It levels the playing field, giving the child a chance at learning to read. As one teacher put it, "He's still struggling and needs to learn the skills he's missed, but at least with his Irlen Filters the words are staying on the page now, and that has to make it easier for him to learn to read!"

One of the main problems we encounter today—with the emphasis being on early intervention and learning the basic skills such as phonics—is that the focus is almost entirely on young readers, up to third grade. However, reading problems are clearly not exclusive to young children and are not only due to problems learning the basic skills.

Given the announcement on the Nation's Report Card from 2006—that two out of every three high school seniors read below grade level—it is clear that America's older students need help improving their reading and writing skills as well. In fact, there is a significant adult population that also struggles to read.

The educational system is finally becoming aware of "later emerging" reading problems that are experienced by students in the upper grades of elementary school and continue throughout their school career and beyond. One can only wonder how many of these older students have Irlen Syndrome. I can't even begin to count the teens and adults who have come to see me with reading difficulties related to fluency and comprehension. One woman who came to see me was eighty-three.

Moving from Learning to Read to Reading to Learn

To understand the plight of the struggling reader whose reading problems do not surface until third grade or later, we need to stop thinking of reading only in terms of being able to read words correctly or read at grade level. Almost every adult who seeks Irlen testing starts out by saying, "I know how to read, but I just don't read."

Reading is complex and requires the acquisition of a variety of different skills, and these skills will change as a person gets older. Initially, children are taught the beginning skills of letter identification, phonics, and word recognition. Usually, by third grade, learning requires that they progress to a different set of skills so that they can read to obtain information. Essentially, this is when children go from *learning to read* to *reading to learn*. At this point, children are required to use their reading skills to read directions, gain information, and answer questions. It is assumed that the basic reading skills have become automatic, especially if the child is reading at grade level. After third grade, we usually no longer hear students read aloud, so we tend to assume that they can read and understand assigned material and that they are able to read for longer periods of time. If there is a problem, teachers assume that repetition and practice will automatically lead to flow, fluency, and comprehension.

Research, however, has shown that this is not the case. Some children continue to read slowly and laboriously throughout their school years, struggling academically, which results in difficulties staying motivated. They are not able to understand and assess academic content, which results in poor grades, poor school achievement, and ultimately affects success in later life. We need to open our eyes and look for a different direction for these struggling readers to take.

Most often, as parents and teachers, we focus on the student's ability to perform in content areas. We think that problems are now related to how well students understand science, history, math, and their other subjects. The focus of the problem moves away from a reading issue and becomes an issue with the student's ability to interpret and understand the material being read.

As children continue from grade school into middle school, the amount of reading does increase; but the educational system puts less emphasis on the need to read in order to pass a course. By listening in class, taking good notes, participating in group discussions or projects, and using CliffsNotes and summations of books found on the internet, reading can be largely avoided or minimized and a student can still do very well in middle school and even high school. Utilizing such strategies makes it easy for many students to move along from grade to grade, doing a minimal amount of reading along the way. For many of these students, Irlen Syndrome will be at the root of their reading difficulties; but, it will likely go undetected, possibly until the student goes to college, where reading requirements make up a significant part of most academic programs. In fact, many students are not even aware that they have a reading problem because they have always been able to pass their courses without reading. In some cases, they were even getting good grades.

When academic problems are recognized beyond grade school, they are rarely ever attributed to reading difficulties. The assumption is made that the student has learned to read and that he must be struggling for other reasons. After all, if you hear about a student having academic difficulty in college, you would probably never think that it was a reading problem.

As a result, students become frustrated, depressed, and, in some cases, may even drop out of college under the belief that they have failed to meet the high expectations that everyone—including themselves—had for them.

Practice Does Not Always "Make Perfect"

One of the most exasperating concepts is that practice makes perfect. It is exasperating because it is not the case if there is a barrier, such as Irlen Syndrome. If you have Irlen Syndrome, the longer you try, the harder it becomes to read. Unfortunately, this concept is most often stressed all throughout the educational system as the way to help struggling readers. One mother discussed her daughter's experiences:

My daughter struggled in first grade learning to read and was placed in the Reading Recovery program. Reading continued to be difficult, and all I kept hearing was, "Have her practice reading more at home." I asked to have her tested, but I was told that her reading problems were not severe. Again I was told that she needed more practice. But practice alone was not helping. I had always felt that there was an underlying reason for her reading problem and kept searching. When I discovered Irlen, it resonated. I had found an answer, not only for my daughter, but also for myself.

—KAREN, IRLEN CLIENT FILES

Since perceptual reading problems are hereditary, parents of children with Irlen Syndrome often have a feeling of "been there, done that." They often see similarities between their reading difficulties and those of their child. Often parents are surprised and delighted during the testing to find help not just for their child, but also for themselves and other family members who may also be struggling.

THE MANY FACES OF THE STRUGGLING READER

Even those learning to read can have Irlen Syndrome. In order to read, a person needs to be able to accurately and consistently see letters before being able to associate letters to sounds. Young children with Irlen Syndrome may confuse letters because they look alike. The most common problems are being able to see the difference between the following lowercase letters:

- b and d
- a, e, o, and u
- m, n, u, and w
- i and l

In addition, some of these children may reverse letters because they are switching around. Obviously, everyone should be taught the basic skills; but imagine how difficult it would be if parts of letters disappeared, flipped, or doubled. If people don't learn to read when they are young, it is reasonable to assume that they will continue to have issues with reading as they get older.

So what else identifies the struggling reader? The schools consider a student reading two grades below grade level to be a struggling reader. However, this isn't always the case for those with Irlen Syndrome. These students can have excellent grades and good reading skills but may also have reading problems. They may need to re-read for comprehension. In other instances, they may experience physical symptoms and stop reading; and because it hurts to read and re-reading takes so long, they avoid reading. These students get caught in the eye of the storm. No one believes they have a problem since they are able to get good grades. Yet, they, too, make up the faces of struggling readers.

Jane is in the gifted program in school. When she was in the tenth grade, she came to me saying that she was having trouble reading, which no one would believe because she had gotten all As on her report card. She knew she had a problem because it took her so long to read her textbooks that she only got two to three hours of sleep at night. Even the school said that she couldn't possibly have a reading problem. What they did not know was how hard she struggled to complete her reading assignments. In fact, for a long time, no one realized how hard she was trying.

—JANET, IRLEN CLIENT FILES

Students who re-read for comprehension or read for a relatively short period of time often have Irlen Syndrome. This is due to what we call the "ten minute factor." Research has shown that many of the problems associated with Irlen Syndrome take effect when the person has been reading (or trying to read) for about ten minutes. Then, the effort and discomfort become too much, and the student finds numerous excuses to stop reading. Typically, the child is then told to pay attention or stop being lazy, and so on. Parents may be told that their child has a short attention span and very often ADD is mentioned.

Difficulties may not be evident until college when it is far more difficult to get around the need to read in order to pass courses. One student who came to see me epitomized so many of the other college students that I see. She tried to get through college using the same strategies that worked for her in high school. But, unlike high school, she could no longer pass her college courses by listening in class and not doing the assigned reading. She had a difficult time with tests and described reading as "overwhelming." However, she told me she thought everyone else was just like her; that everyone else would also begin to feel tired if they read for longer than a few minutes.

After the first semester of college, she dropped out and went home. She had no idea that she was trying to read pages where the words were going in and out of focus, disappearing, and pulsating up and down. If that wasn't bad enough, the white page glowed and competed with the print for her attention. Fortunately, she found out about the Irlen Method and came in for testing. Now she wears Irlen Filters, which allowed her to return to school.

Dyslexia

You cannot talk about reading problems without mentioning dyslexia. Often, the terms "reading disabilities" and "dyslexia" are used inter-changeably. Dyslexia has different meanings depending on whom you ask, but most agree that it is a lifelong disorder that cannot be helped with standard instruction because the underlying cause is unknown. The educational system, parents, and certain professional groups use the term differently. In fact, the educational system does not recognize dyslexia and will, instead, label children with severe reading issues as "learning disabled." Or, they may simply not acknowledge the problem at all if the student in question is getting good grades.

Some professionals believe that dyslexia is a disconnection between the print on the page and the brain, resulting in an inability to process information visually. This can cause difficulty with recognition of letters and words. It can also cause difficulty acquiring sight vocabulary (words the reader immediately recognizes without having to sound out) and problems processing information efficiently and accurately.

For the most part, parents agree with this opinion. They tend to believe that dyslexia holds their child back from making progress, even with practice, instruction, and remediation.

Other professional groups define dyslexia as a language-based prob-lem affecting reading and other aspects of oral language. These groups believe treatment requires a specific type of teaching with an emphasis on phonics.

In the end, there is a general consensus that those with dyslexia have a type of processing difficulty, although professionals cannot seem to agree on a single definition or cause. Therefore, parents need to be open to various causes and possible interventions, one of which may be the Irlen Method.

THINGS PARENTS CAN DO TO HELP

Approximately 45 percent of students who have reading problems, dyslexia, or learning difficulties actually have Irlen Syndrome and are being misdiagnosed. For this type of struggling reader, you'll want to pay close attention to the reading habits of your child and see if there is a pattern. (For misconceptions about reading, see page 76.) A child may simply not be in the mood to read on a given night, but an ongoing pat-tern indicates a problem. On the next page, there are a few questions you may want to ask yourself.

Does your child:

- Complain of headaches, feel tired, or exhibit other physical symptoms when reading or while doing homework?

- Have attention, motivational, or behavioral problems while reading?

- Have difficulty with reading despite showing good reading skills?

- Have problems with comprehension?

- Have trouble tracking from line to line?

- Lose his place often?

- Read the same word differently from one time to the next?

- Read words better in isolation than on a page?

- Show no adequate progress with instruction or remediation?

Misconceptions About Reading

There are some common misconceptions about reading that are widely shared. They include:

- All problems seeing print can be corrected with glasses.
- Black print on a white background is the best contrast for reading.
- Everyone can easily read for an hour or longer.
- Everyone can see groups of words clearly.
- Everyone sees letters, words, and numbers the same way.
- Good reading skills are all that are needed to read.
- Letters and words are always seen as having spaces between them.
- People who can't read aren't trying.
- The print always remains still and never moves.
- The print is always clear and never changes.
- The print always stands out and is more dominant than the background.
- Reading never gives people headaches or makes them sleepy.
- White paper always looks white.

Making these assumptions or believing these misconceptions can result in overlooking a perceptual problem.

Answering "yes" to one or more of those questions (not necessarily all of them) indicates that your child may be struggling to read because of Irlen Syndrome.

As discussed, students who are doing well in school may be struggling readers. Approximately 12 to 14 percent of the general population falls into this category.

To determine if your child is a part of this statistic, try to notice if he:

- Avoids reading, especially reading for pleasure.

- Does poorly on timed or standardized tests.

- Has problems keeping attention or staying motivated.

- Is easily distracted.

- Learns from listening in class rather than doing assigned reading.

- Re-reads for comprehension.

- Reads beginnings and endings, or summaries, rather than reading the entire chapter.

- Reads in dim lighting.

- Shows a discrepancy between reading and other skills.

- Spends excessive time completing homework assignments.

- Studies notes from class rather than doing the assigned reading.

- Uses CliffsNotes or summaries of books from the internet.

- Works hard to get good grades but feels that he is brighter than the grades indicate.

Reading for pleasure is not the same as reading textbooks. I have had so many parents whose children appeared to have good reading skills say to me, "My child can't have a reading problem. He has read all of the *Harry Potter* books." It is important to take into account that pleasure reading requires vastly different skills than textbook reading, since many paperbacks are printed on off-white paper (which helps with contrast) and, when reading for pleasure, you can skip-read and still follow the story. There is also no timeframe or deadline with pleasure reading, so if your son or daughter reads a little at a time before feeling tired or falling asleep, nobody will know the difference. Therefore, pleasure reading is not as good an indicator of your child's ability to read for information.

Since it is difficult to know if your child is having problems, you can find out a lot of information by asking a few simple questions. However, before you ask, you need to make it clear what you are looking for—make sure your child knows you are referring to reading textbooks and that you are not talking about when he starts reading, but rather how he feels when he stops. Then ask the following questions.

- How do you, your eyes, and your head feel?

- How does the page look to you?

- Is it easier to read in bright light, dim light, or does it make no difference?

- Is it easier to read under the lighting at home, at school, or does it make no difference?

If your child's answers reflect a stable and clear page and no physical symptoms, then you are likely not dealing with Irlen Syndrome. However, if he reports that the page changes, the words move, reading becomes uncomfortable after more than a few minutes, or that it is much harder to read under the fluorescent lights at school, then you should consider having him tested. Also, keep in mind that it may not be the print that is causing the problem but the white background. Even if the print stays clear and doesn't move, there still may be an issue. Finally, if your child manages to avoid reading, asking these questions is futile because he does not read long enough to experience the real problems.

BRAIN STUDIES ON READING

How important is the perceptual aspect of reading? Brain studies have provided some very interesting findings. Functional neuroimaging techniques have been used to study individuals labeled as having reading difficulties. The individuals who were studied had also been diagnosed with Irlen Syndrome.

These scans provide a dynamic snapshot of what the brain looks like, indicating blood flow and/or brain activation. Results have suggested that the processing of printed material is accompanied by higher-than-expected levels of activation in certain areas of the brain. This means that the brain is working harder than it should, making it less effective at processing information from a printed page. This validates that certain types of reading problems and dyslexia can stem from perception difficulties.

When the brain cannot accurately process visual information, the individual may be mislabeled as having learning problems, reading difficulties, or as being hyperactive. When underlying problems of this nature are not identified, the result may be children with social, emotional, and/or academic problems.

One woman who has a university degree never reads unless it is absolutely necessary, because, as she puts it, "It's like trying to read raindrops running down a windowpane." People with Irlen Syndrome perceive the page, the print, and sometimes the environment differently. Their brains have to constantly adapt and compensate. The individual is unaware of the huge strain his brain is under and the colossal energy needed to complete a perceptual task. With all the mental effort going into perceiving and processing, comprehension becomes impossible. Children and adults do not know why they stop reading, they just know they have to stop.

One mother explained her son's pain.

He wouldn't look at the page but would, instead, push it off to the side like he wasn't trying. I would read to him and write his answers down. The school had no idea why he couldn't read. They told me that they were sorry, but they didn't know what was wrong or how to fix it. What no one knew or asked was how Ryan saw the page. The words moved together without any spacing in-between. He never saw individual words. If that wasn't bad enough, when he looked at the page, his eyes would water and hurt. He experienced frequent headaches and would sometimes actually get nauseous. His brain was working overtime to process the words, and it was causing him great pain.

—CONNIE, IRLEN CLIENT FILES

CONCLUSION

Instruction—whether with phonics, linguistics, or other methods—along with practice, may not be the answer for all struggling readers. This will not always result in enhancing flow, fluency, attention, comfort, and comprehension for those students with Irlen Syndrome. Therefore, there is a compelling reason to look beyond and find out whether there are more basic causes that need to be addressed first. Whether the problem is labeled as a learning difficulty, reading problem, or dyslexia, perceptual difficulties related to distortions and discomfort can be an underlying barrier preventing children (and adults) from being able to use reading skills to learn. The Irlen Method allows the individual to read effortlessly, thus focusing on the *meaning* of what is being read instead of the actual task of reading.

In no way do I want to diminish the importance of reading instruction. I fully support the need for instruction and remediation, but any underlying roadblocks need to be taken care of first. Think of perception as the building block to being able to learn and being able to use the skills you have been taught. Before building a bridge, you would want to make sure it had a solid foundation. In the same manner, you want your child to have the basic foundation in place for reading. For example, you would not expect your child to read without correcting any visual problems. Glasses for better vision would not teach your child to read, but would allow him to utilize skills as they are learned. Following the same logic, why would you expect your child to read without first correcting the problems with his brain's ability to accurately process visual information? Think of the eye as the camera lens and the brain as the photo developer. You need to make sure that both are working correctly in order to get your photos. The same holds true with reading—both vision and perception need to be working correctly to achieve the desired results. Schools also need to incorporate screening for Irlen Syndrome by providing students with the inexpensive colored overlays before utilizing other costly interventions.

In the next chapter, we will look at other areas—such as depth perception—that are affected by Irlen Syndrome. The chapter will describe the different types of distortions that cause poor depth perception and the various activities that are affected.

6

Irlen Syndrome Goes
Beyond the Printed Page

Ginny would constantly run into everything. She tripped all the time and just thought she was a big klutz. She couldn't tell distance and had trouble determining how close or far away things were from her. When reaching for a doorknob, she couldn't grab it without hitting it first. She saw things as clumped together and had to feel an item to tell if it was round or flat. Mountains looked like flat triangles, and the sun looked like it was flat and round. She was scared to death to change lanes while driving because she would often unintentionally cut off other cars, even though she was sure she had more than enough room.

—GINNY, IRLEN CLIENT FILES

For Ginny, and many others with Irlen Syndrome, reading was only part of the problem. Irlen Filters helped Ginny, but clearly not just with reading. In this chapter, we will begin to move away from the printed page and start discussing the many other problems that make life more challenging for many of the people with Irlen Syndrome.

From our initial success with Irlen Filters, making reading easier and more comfortable for so many people who had struggled for years, we received thousands of letters and phone calls of thanks from people all over the world.

Hearing about the changes from so many adults and children who were wearing Irlen Filters was very gratifying. It was also very eye-opening. Many of the cards and letters we received spoke of improvements with not only reading, but other areas as well. We were hearing from people that it was not just the flashing, moving letters or distortions on the page that made reading so difficult, but that it had physically hurt to read. Along with being able to read comfortably, headaches, fatigue, and physical symptoms that people never thought much about—or for which they had compensated—were also suddenly gone. The thrill of not having to accept headaches as a part of life was an awakening for people who had suffered silently for so long. The excitement from adults who could now do things they could never do before was evident as they happily told us about the changes they were experiencing. From our clients, we learned that physical symptoms could also disappear with Irlen Filters.

When people came back for filter checks, they, too, reported improvements in other areas of life aside from reading. Story after story repeated the same positive results, all taking us beyond the printed page. In time, we used this information to identify a wide range of problems that improved with Irlen Spectral Filters. These problems included light sensitivity, headaches and migraines, sports performance, and depth perception. In addition, individuals with diagnoses including ADD, ADHD, certain medical and visual issues, head injuries, psychological issues, or those on the autism spectrum found that they also had Irlen-like symptoms which were eliminated with Irlen Filters (all are discussed in the following chapters).

"I NEVER KNEW THERE WAS A SOLUTION"

Many people did not seek solutions simply because they were not even aware that there was a problem. These problems are different from reading in that they are ones people typically find ways to circumvent, accept, or ignore. If, for example, your trouble was with reading music, you could simply stop taking music lessons. If you couldn't catch or hit a ball, you might just assume that you simply aren't very good at sports. If you were always bumping into things or tripping, you could label yourself as clumsy, laugh at your missteps, and accept that clumsiness is part of who you are. If you get headaches at work, you might just assume they are simply stress-related; or if other people in your family also get frequent headaches, you could assume it is normal. If driving at night bothers you, it's easy to avoid. The point is, many people compensate for their difficulties rather than address them. Reading, however, is different. It is important for success in school and in life, so it's much harder to ignore reading difficulties. Teachers and parents typically see such difficulties; although, as mentioned in the previous chapter, many people try using strategies to compensate in that area as well, typically with limited success as they mature into adulthood.

Our clients—especially the adults—led the way to understanding and documenting the various areas of life besides reading that improved with the use of Irlen Filters. They showed us the power of color and helped identify the exact problems and areas that could be changed for the better by using the Irlen Method. While there was not a 100 percent correlation between having Irlen Syndrome and physical symptoms, a very high percentage of our clients reported some type of physical symptom, discomfort, strain, or fatigue with triggers being lighting, computers, reading, and/or other academic tasks. Additionally, we then started hearing numerous stories about the improvements people experienced in non-academic tasks, such as driving a car or simply walking up or down a flight of stairs.

The upcoming chapters of this book will allow you to connect the dots and find out for yourself how many different and separate problems are related to one issue—Irlen Syndrome. It should not come as a surprise since the root of Irlen Syndrome is a perceptual processing problem. Why would reading be the only processing difficulty? It makes sense that anything that we look at could also be affected in the same way, with distortions and, for some, physical symptoms. Since the brain processes visual information, it can, therefore, result in a wide range of perceptual problems.

ENVIRONMENTAL FACTORS

Initially, we had no idea the environment had such an impact on Irlen Syndrome because nobody talked about the environment affecting how they felt and performed. Feeling tired and exhausted after school or work, feeling anxious and avoiding shopping in certain stores, or sitting in a classroom or at work being unable to focus or concentrate is typically chalked up to stress or a lack of sleep. Rarely does someone consider the source of the problem to be the environment around them.

Today, we are very aware that one of the most common areas of concern for those with Irlen Syndrome is headaches that result from a sensitivity to light (for an in-depth discussion on this topic, see Chapter 7 on page 91). In addition, many people with Irlen Syndrome reported that it was difficult for them to see fluorescent colors and patterns. In fact, some clients talked about problems looking at wallpaper, clothing, and carpets. It's all a matter of perception. For one person, the wallpaper may look colorful and full of great designs, but for another, it may be nearly impossible to look at without feeling dizzy or getting a headache. Visual perception varies from person to person. For example, you may have noticed that when a newscaster or someone on television wears a brightly colored tie or shirt, it may seem to sparkle, glare, or "bleed" as they say in the television industry. For this reason, people are instructed not to wear certain colors or patterns when they go in front of the camera. For some people with Irlen Syndrome, these symptoms occur daily, both on the TV and in life.

I've heard many examples of environmental factors affecting children and adults with Irlen Syndrome. I remember that "ah-ha!" moment during testing when one parent suddenly made the connection between her child having trouble falling asleep at night and the new wallpaper she had put in the child's room. Once, during testing, when the parent heard the child say that the words moved on the page, she asked her child about the new wallpaper. She replied that she was frightened by the horses on the wallpaper because they kept running around the room. I also recall a woman who bought a new house that had lots of large windows with wonderful views overlooking the water. She loved the house until she moved in and started getting headaches all the time. When she came in to see us, the questions during the testing made her realize that she was getting constant headaches from the brightness and the glare coming in from all of those windows.

In general, many people are sensitive to their environments. Some people are sensitive to certain smells, such as strong perfumes. Others get headaches from the markers used to write on whiteboards. Still others can hear the high-pitched buzz of fluorescent lights. But since these factors only affect a small percentage of people, those people typically become used to living with these problems, accept them as normal, and rarely complain. Likewise, for those with Irlen Syndrome, certain visuals can be over-stimulating, creating the same type of problems in a number of environments. Hotels, for example, put down carpeting with patterns in the rooms so that they will know where to put the furniture. Some of those patterns can be extremely distorting, disturbing, and disorientating to someone with Irlen Syndrome.

The world is largely unaware of sensory sensitivities. Teachers send home important notices on fluorescent-colored paper and use fluorescent-colored markers on whiteboards. Additionally, many schools are replacing green boards with whiteboards, designing windowless classrooms, and using bright yellow or bright white paint on the walls. One school had the misguided concept of using white walls, white desks, and white floors. As a result, the number of students experiencing and complaining of headaches rose significantly.

Rectifying the Issues

In order to assist, we need to deal with all of these environmental problems and the issues that create them. Unfortunately, since it is a minority of individuals who suffer, problems go largely unnoticed by those who are planning, building, and designing the environments in which we live. Rather than recognizing that some people cannot function normally under very bright lights, the lighting in schools and offices keeps getting brighter. In fact, lighting today is more than twice as bright as it was prior to World War II.[1-3] What this means is that the amount of candlepower that lighting engineers have decided is optimal has literally doubled from the 1950s to the early years of the twenty-first century, under the premise that brighter is better.

Can you control your environment? As discussed earlier, you can avoid certain areas that give you difficulty. For example, one woman who came to see me told me how she stopped shopping at a particular store because the lighting was too bright. Unaware of the actual problem, she found other stores in which to shop. Another client left her high school teaching job because of the headaches she had every day from the fluorescent lights that the principal wouldn't let her turn off.

The bottom line is while you *can* change the wallpaper in your child's room or put drapes over windows to lessen the amount of light coming into the house, there are many situations in which you *cannot* control your environment. The stories from people who were found to have Irlen Syndrome and, subsequently, wore Irlen Filters provided us with positive feedback regarding the ways the Irlen Method made it possible to function normally in environments that used to be problematic.

DEPTH PERCEPTION

"I have Irlen Syndrome," explains a high school senior. "I noticed I had a problem when I started driving. Passing other vehicles when there was another car coming made me very nervous, but my mom encouraged me to pass. Afterwards she would explain that the car was still a mile away. I just couldn't tell."

—JIM, IRLEN CLIENT FILES

Depth perception problems are typically considered to be visual problems related to binocularity difficulties, which means the two eyes are not working together. Depth perception requires both binocular cues (input from both eyes) and monocular cues (input from just one eye). Although vision specialists usually consider binocular difficulties to be the cause of poor depth perception, many individuals with Irlen Syndrome do not see a three-dimensional picture because the brain is inaccurately processing monocular cues. Therefore, an area in which we have seen great improvement with the Irlen Method is depth perception. No, people don't come in and say their depth perception is better; they do, however, describe specific activities that are easier for them to do after having been treated for Irlen Syndrome, areas in life that they had not necessarily acknowledged as problems. For example, many people will make jokes about bumping into things, their inability to catch a ball, or about how everyone yells at them when they knock over and spill things. They'll joke about being clumsy but do not realize that depth perception issues may be at the root of their difficulties. For example, some clients used to wait and wait before making a left turn, even though everyone in the car was yelling to go. Wearing Irlen Spectral Filters, they are now able to make the turns without waiting for traffic to be completely clear. Likewise, our clients who would stand in front of an escalator nervously trying to gauge when to get on, or simply took elevators from floor to floor instead, have reported that escalators are no longer a problem.

In most cases, depth perception issues are problems that people compensate for, usually without ever thinking about them. One client told me she had to ask someone else to bring her child on the escalator because she needed to hold onto the railing and did not have enough hands to hold her packages and her child's hand at the same time. Another client told me that she memorized the number of steps it took her to walk from location to location in her house and was careful not to move the furniture so she would not bump into things. As mentioned, you *can* control some degree of your environment. In regard to the depth perception problems just discussed, most people did exactly that, controlling what they could within their environment and avoiding what they could not control.

For those with Irlen Syndrome, depth perception problems involve difficulties with how the brain processes visual information, causing things to look different. A variety of activities that require the ability to accurately judge distance and spatial relationships between objects are affected. Some people with Irlen Syndrome experience difficulties in sports performance—catching, throwing, hitting, or kicking a ball; or jumping or tracking moving objects. Other individuals with Irlen Syndrome have trouble navigating through spaces, typically ones in which there are turns or objects to maneuver around.

Some common symptoms of depth perception issues affect the way an individual sees objects. The list on the next page explains some common occurrences with this issue (and the inset below can help you recognize if you have a depth perception issue).

Recognizing Depth Perception Issues

Here are some questions to consider that may help you recognize some depth perception issues that can can be helped with Irlen Filters.

When driving, do you:

- Experience difficulty maneuvering into a parking space?
- Feel like you are going to hit the car in front of you?
- Feel uncertain when switching lanes?
- Have difficulty judging when to make a turn in front of cars?
- Have difficulty judging whether you can navigate through a narrow area?
- Leave more space than necessary between your car and the car ahead of you?

When playing sports, do you:

- Have problems tracking a ball or other moving objects?
- Have trouble catching or hitting a ball?
- Have trouble judging when to jump when playing jump rope?

When walking, do you:

- Drift into the person next to you?
- Frequently bump into things, such as table edges or door jambs?
- Frequently knock things over?
- Have difficulty getting on or off escalators?
- Consider yourself clumsy?
- Have difficulty stepping on or off curbs?
- Have difficulty walking up or down stairs?

If you have a depth perception issue, objects can:

- Appear and disappear

- Appear blurry

- Appear in bits and pieces

- Appear to be flat and not 3-D

- Appear to be moving, sometimes at varying speeds

- Look closer than they really are

Some of the most emotional reactions we get are from adults who, with their Irlen Filters, see their world in 3-D for the very first time. It is such a shock and so overwhelming that they often burst into tears. They are seeing individual leaves rather than a clump of color; the space between trees; the way the curb is higher than the road; the contours of someone's face; or the doorknob sticking out from the door—and these are only some of the changes.

A college professor who came to us to be tested for Irlen Syndrome recounts her story:

I now understand why I had such difficulty learning cross country skiing even though I knew I was coordinated. I now know why I crashed into furniture, banged my head so many times on shelves, hit corners, and generally felt clumsy even though I am not. My perception of 3-D was actually a layered 2-D, like a stage set. I was seeing the world in a series of flat images. Finally, I had an explanation as to why I couldn't catch a ball unless I concentrated really hard—I had no idea where the thrown object was in space.

—TERRY, IRLEN CLIENT FILES

Misdiagnosis

Kathryn was told she had a panic disorder. She took Zanax and Paxil but still suffered with anxiety. She felt unsafe and exhausted outside of her home. Shopping was very difficult. She could not find things on the shelves as they were moving and disappearing under the bright lights; and she quickly became sweaty, weak, felt faint, and had to leave.

Kathryn even panicked when riding in a car. Whenever her hus-band stopped at a traffic light, she felt like they were going to drive into the car in front of them. When a car turned in front of them, she felt as if it was going to drive into them. She was constantly holding on to the door handles and found it frightening to look at the traffic.

Once she was tested for Irlen Syndrome and given Irlen Filters, Kathryn's panic and anxiety disappeared as the world around her no longer appeared distorted.

—KATHRYN, IRLEN CLIENT FILES

Often, by the time people come to see us, they have already been misdi-agnosed. Some individuals with Irlen Syndrome have such severe depth perception problems that getting from place to place is almost impossi-ble. A few Irlen clients with very poor depth perception are misdiag-nosed with anxiety and panic disorder. Thus, the problem does not get better with commonly-prescribed anxiety medications or over-the-counter products because neither the individual nor the doctor is aware that the problem lies in that connection between the eyes and the brain.

CONCLUSION

While most people seek us out because of reading problems, we are now aware of the wide range of issues and physical symptoms that someone with Irlen Syndrome may experience. It has allowed us to expand our knowledge base and our awareness of the wide array of areas that can be affected. It has also alerted us to the problems created by certain aspects of our daily environment and how, if anything, the ongoing emphasis on "brighter" lighting and poor depth perception continue to compound such problems.

In the next chapter, we will take a closer look at lighting and how it has become a serious issue for many people; an issue that continues to remain largely unrecognized.

7

Light Sensitivity and Irlen Syndrome

For as long as I can remember, I have been bothered by bright lights—especially those darn fluorescent lights they use in schools. For years, I have felt ill working at my desk under those lights and, at times, have felt incapable of getting anything accomplished. Even though I am a reading teacher, I sometimes find reading difficult under fluorescent lights. After reading for awhile, the print becomes blurred and even sometimes begins to move around on the page.

Driving can be frightening because of the glare from the other cars' headlights. Shopping, believe it or not, is also sometimes a challenge because I can't see colors under the lighting, and I feel the need to shade my eyes.

This year, through a colleague of mine, I discovered that my problems—which I really believed everyone experienced—were not shared by everyone. In fact, my colleague offered to test me for something called Irlen Syndrome. Not only was it confirmed that I have Irlen Syndrome, but I have since become a certified screener. You could say that for me, finding out about the Irlen Method was truly an eye-opening experience.

—MICHAEL, IRLEN CLIENT FILES

The above is just one of several letters you will read in this chapter that focuses on the problems created by (and subsequent concerns about) lighting. Light sensitivity, also referred to as photophobia, is a serious issue for millions of people, not only those with Irlen Syndrome but also for those with lupus, epilepsy, chronic fatigue syndrome, and various other health issues. It is a condition that extends to bright overhead lights, movie theatre screens, computer screens, streetlights, automobile headlights, and especially fluorescent lighting (which will be discussed in greater detail shortly). When light sensitivity is severe, the individuals who suffer from it have problems functioning in many different environments. Whether it is caused by sunlight, indoor lighting, car headlights, taillights, or glare, light sensitivity is a significant area of concern—one that can pervade all areas of life. (For signs of light sensitivity, see the inset on page 95.)

VERY LITTLE LIGHT SHED ON THE SUBJECT

Light sensitivity is a subject that is often overlooked. It is not recognized as potentially having dire consequences, nor is it recognized by the educational system or given serious attention by most medical professionals. Therefore, most individuals who suffer from light sensitivity continue to live and cope with the symptoms. Often they compensate, never realizing that they have a problem and that their quality of life could be so much better if they wore Irlen Spectral Filters. (Light sensitivity is not exclusive to those with Irlen Syndrome, and even non-Irlen sufferers who have light sensitivity issues can benefit from Irlen Filters).

Many people associate light sensitivity only with sunlight. However, it would be of greater benefit to many people if the definition of light sensitivity was expanded to include sensitivity to bright indoor lighting, fluorescent lighting, headlights, streetlights, and even the resulting glare from various sources of light.

To put it simply, light sensitivity is a problem—a real problem—that should not be dismissed. Yet, since the majority of the population is not bothered by light sensitivity, environments are continually created with an emphasis on bright light. This is not good for some people since the invisible symptoms of light sensitivity can be pretty severe. Headaches, migraines, stomachaches, dizziness, sleepiness, fatigue, anxiety, irritability, and even a fight-or-flight response (similar to a panic attack) are some of the symptoms that accompany light sensitivity.

ACQUIRED VS. INHERITED

Light sensitivity may be inherited as a symptom of Irlen Syndrome, but you need not have Irlen Syndrome to suffer from light sensitivity. There are various other triggers for light sensitivity or photophobia. Such sensitivity may be acquired as the result of certain medical or visual conditions. Glaucoma, lupus, epilepsy, and autoimmune diseases can result in light sensitivity, as can allergic reactions and reactions to medications like birth control pills. If light sensitivity continues to be a problem after treatment for your medical condition, the Irlen Method may be a viable option for addressing this problem—even if you do not have Irlen Syndrome.

If you do not have Irlen Syndrome but are light sensitive, you can still be helped by the Irlen Method and Irlen Spectral Filters. Remember, Irlen Filters will alleviate the struggles with light sensitivity and improve your quality of life but will not cure an illness or medical condition, which should be handled by a medical doctor.

Irlen Filters can also take away the stress and physical symptoms that can result from lighting, thus eliminating not only the light sensitivity, but also the ensuing headaches, fatigue, or other physical symptoms. (To learn more about Irlen Spectral Filters as a way of minimizing Irlen-like symptoms, go to Chapter 11 on page 145).

Regardless of whether this problem is inherited or acquired, the symptoms can range from mild to serious.

MAKING MATTERS WORSE

As noted earlier, the brightness of lighting has more than doubled since the inception of fluorescent lighting. As a result—and contradictory to the common assumption "brighter is better"—we have seen a marked increase in the number of people feeling sick, exhausted, and experiencing physical symptoms. Much of this is due to the widespread use of fluorescent lighting in schools, offices, stores, and public buildings. In fact, fluorescent lighting is even being used as backlighting for some new computer screens.

As if that weren't enough, there is a movement throughout parts of the world (including here in the United States) to ban incandescent light bulbs and replace them with, primarily, compact fluorescent light bulbs (CFL bulbs). This is in order to save energy. Australia recently enacted a law that banned most sales of incandescent light bulbs by 2010. Likewise, Canada announced a similar plan to phase out the sale of incandescent bulbs by 2012. The Finnish parliament has also been discussing a ban on incandescent light bulbs, which would start by the beginning of 2011. And right here in the United States, there is talk of taking similar steps by 2012.

While these new laws do not specify that CFL bulbs are to be used as replacements, CFL bulbs are being highly marketed as the alternative from an energy-saving perspective. In fact, some major chain stores have already started committing heavily to CFL bulbs. In 2008, Walmart announced that it is looking to sell 100 million of these bulbs over the next several years.

The problem with banning incandescent lights and increasing marketing of CFLs is that while helping the environment is a worthwhile endeavor, in this case it is at the expense of many people. Estimates now show that nearly one-quarter of the world's population suffer from health issues that can be related to fluorescent lights. For this portion of the population, fluorescent lights trigger headaches, migraines, stomachaches, fatigue, eye strain, and other symptoms. Fluorescent lights can negatively impact the immune system, literally making people sick. Additionally, they may also interfere with reading, writing, attention, concentration, and the ability to learn and perform.

Eliminating incandescent lights would be like removing elevators from five story buildings to save electricity. Think, however, of the serious implications removing elevators would have for those who cannot walk stairs. A ban on these bulbs will truly leave many people in the dark.

I am a fifty-five year old adult, and I have a long history of working around fluorescent lights. As a teenager and young adult, going to the market with my mother or on my own was a major trial. We now know that the lights in public places—markets, office buildings, malls, stores, and schools—were the cause of behavioral and physical changes for my mother, two of my sisters, and myself. Being in buildings with these lights would cause us to get headaches within minutes. Our eyes would hurt, or we would get upset stomachs and become anxious and short-tempered.

At times as an adult, the lighting in the supermarket would be so annoying and upset me so much that I would actually walk away from my cart full of food and cry all the way to my car. Because of this, our family started using strategies. Even though we did not know why, we would just get the shopping done as fast as possible by splitting up the list. Each of us would find a few items and bring them back to the cart, thus cutting the time spent in the market in half.

When I became older and started working in offices or in retail stores, I found I was unable to handle stressful situations, mainly because I was always tense under the lights.

—STACEY, IRLEN CLIENT FILES

As Stacey mentions in her letter, she and her family would come up with strategies, such as dividing up and hurrying through the shopping, to avoid spending extended amounts of time under fluorescent lighting. Unfortunately, these strategies cannot compensate for the myriad of places in which lighting will have an effect on someone with light sensitivity.

Signs of Light Sensitivity

Both children and adults can be light sensitive. This list contains some of the signs. Do you or your child:

- Avoid driving at night?
- Become antsy or wiggly in fluorescent lights?
- Become sleepy when driving or as a passenger?
- Change behavior (get more irritable or cranky) when in places with fluorescent lights, such as classrooms or stores?
- Close eyes, look away, or squint when someone is taking a flash picture?
- Feel bothered by glare even on cloudy days?
- Feel bothered by headlights from other cars?
- Get a headache or become tired in fluorescent lights?
- Read or do schoolwork in dim lighting?
- Prefer shade to being in sunshine and seek out shady areas?
- Prefer to wear a hat or sunglasses outside and sometimes inside?
- Seem bothered by the sun when riding in a car?
- Sneeze in sunlight?
- Squint when going outside?
- Turn off lights or simply not turn on lights in a room?

If you repeatedly notice some of the items on the list, it is very possible you or your child may have light sensitivity. Many people have told me that if you have blue eyes, you are more light sensitive than others. This is a myth, so worry less about eye color and more about ongoing symptoms or changes of behavior, especially those that occur in places with fluorescent lights. The cause might be Irlen Syndrome, but there are other things that can cause light sensitivity, including medications you or your child may be taking. Explore the various possibilities.

The one place that people have been able to control their environment (at least in terms of lighting) has been in their homes. If legislation to take away incandescent light bulbs is passed, this safe haven where people can remain in control of lighting will be jeopardized.

People who need Irlen Filters are already at a distinct disadvantage in schools and offices because of fluorescent lighting. These people stress and tire quickly. For many, their reading ability quickly deteriorates, and they are no longer productive. If incandescent bulbs are no longer available and they are forced to use fluorescent bulbs in their homes, the same issues will adversely affect their home life.

LIGHT SENSITIVITY, THE BRAIN, AND THE IRLEN METHOD

While this book will not go into great detail about the workings of the brain, it is important to understand how the brain functions under fluorescent lighting and how symptoms of Irlen Syndrome originate.

First, you should know that the brain does *not* perceive light from different sources in different ways. Sunlight, bright lights, headlights, fluorescent lights, streetlights, brake lights, and so on are all perceived by the brain in the same way. Therefore, you can experience the same problems (and physical symptoms) from each of these sources of light. Likewise, the brain perceives the brightness from white paper, whiteboards, computer monitors, and television sets in the same way as it perceives light. This means that the physical symptoms someone with Irlen Syndrome or light sensitivity would experience in bright sunlight and the rest of the situations mentioned are very similar or the same.

However, most of us are aware that sunlight and glare are problems and, as a result, make accommodations such as wearing sunglasses or brimmed hats. In the other situations, many of which are indoors, the brain also responds in the same manner—but we remain unaware of the problems that light, glare, and brightness are creating and, therefore, do not protect ourselves inside like we do on a sunny day.

LIGHT SENSITIVITY AND FATIGUE

Fatigue seems to be a relatively common symptom of light sensitivity. However, most people who have light sensitivity are not aware of this connection and just accept the fact that they tire easily. Children, and even adolescents, may come home from school and take a nap. Adults may crash after work. Some people report falling asleep under the lights in church, and not because they think the preacher is boring. These same individuals wake up and have lots of energy when it gets darker—outside or inside. They may refer to themselves as "night owls," but there is a legitimate reason for the change in their behavior.

LIGHT SENSITIVITY AND CHRONIC STRESS

Women's magazines, as well as health magazines, frequently publish articles warning people of the negative effects of stress (especially chronic stress), giving tips and hints as to how to avoid it. Many of these articles intend to increase awareness of the physical and emotional problems that may result from chronic stress.

Chronic stress is a state of ongoing physiological arousal from repeated stress triggers. The nervous system does not have an opportunity to relax. There can be any number of factors that lead to chronic stress: emotional triggers, such as a bad marriage or high-pressure job, or even environmental factors, such as light sensitivity. As noted by Yellen and Schweller (see page 99), when someone suffers from light sensitivity, it is similar to that person being exposed to constant flashbulbs going off. This does not allow the brain to reset or activate a relaxation response, resulting in chronic stress to the brain. Realize that if you are light sensitive, all lighting—not just fluorescent lighting—is stressful.

While many people are aware of the importance of reducing emotional stress, they rarely take into account environmental factors, such as lighting, as the cause of their physical and emotional problems. Remember, people who have light sensitivity are under constant chronic stress unless their eyes are closed. Those with severe light sensitivity will eventually pay a price, just as anyone suffering from ongoing stress would. Illnesses, fatigue, and possibly even physical symptoms will be the results.

IMPROVEMENTS WITH THE IRLEN METHOD

Laura is sixty years old and used to have difficulty driving at night but never knew why. She had to look away from the oncoming lights or her eyes would hurt and start to tear. It was not just the headlights that were the problem. The red, yellow, and green of the stoplights had halos or extra images when she looked at them. She would also get very tired driving at night, so she would stay in the slow lane, forcing drivers to go around her. This also got rid of the headlights

*reflecting in her rearview mirror. Like most people, she didn't know
it could be different until she was fitted for Irlen Filters. Today, Laura
says that at sixty she is much more comfortable driving at night then
she was back when she was forty.*

—LAURA, IRLEN CLIENT FILES

While most of the people who first came to us to be tested for Irlen Syndrome had reading problems, we found evidence early on that lighting and brightness were also factors to be concerned about. For example, we heard from many parents that their children were reading in dim lighting at home. These parents were always turning on the lights because they had been told that reading in dim lights would hurt their children's eyes. What no one seemed to understand was that the combination of high contrast (black print on white paper) and bright lighting made it more difficult for their children to read. The children dimmed the lights to minimize the contrast, compensating for their difficulties and unknowingly limiting the over-stimulation of their brains.

After we diagnosed and treated these people, many of them—adults, parents, and children—came back and told us about the improvements in their ability to function under fluorescent or bright lights when they were wearing their Irlen Filters. We quickly realized that the filters were helping people who suffered from light sensitivity, whether or not these people had Irlen Syndrome. As a result, we started adding questions about lighting to the Irlen Self-Test so that people would realize that this is a real problem that needs to be addressed.

One common area of concern that we found was driving at night. The contrast between the bright lights from cars and streetlights and the dark night was very difficult for people with Irlen Syndrome and for people with light sensitivity. Some people told us they simply did not drive at night unless they were wearing their Irlen Filters. One client told me that the lights on the dashboard were so bright she had them disconnected. Another client described seeing the brake lights on the cars in front of her as millions and millions of tiny Christmas lights, which made it very hard to tell how close or far away she was from the actual cars.

Other Ways to Help

Since children are rarely aware of light sensitivity, and Irlen Syndrome is hereditary, one thing parents can do to help is try some personal experimentation. For example, they can compare what it's like and how it feels to be in a dimly lit room, in natural lighting, or under fluorescent lighting such as in a store like Target or Walmart. Then, parents should ask themselves the following questions.

- Am I bothered by the lighting?

- Am I getting a headache after being in this environment?

- Do I feel fidgety or nervous?

- Do my eyes hurt?

After answering the questions, parents should leave the environment and see if the symptoms lessen or go away. By stopping to do a self-assessment, parents can determine whether or not different types of lighting affect them. If they are affected, it may hold true that the lighting will have a similar effect on their child.

As parents, understanding how *you* feel in different environmental situations can help you understand how your child feels in similar situations. This can prove to be very beneficial when it comes to a proper diagnosis because parents can relate better and understand what their child is feeling if they are also experiencing (or have experienced) the same thing.

BRAIN STUDIES

Advanced technologies that allow us to study the brain in new and different ways have made the discovery of the unexplainable phenomenon of Irlen Syndrome much more objective. What was once thought of as a figment of someone's imagination is now explainable by both science and technology.

Brain Research and Scans

Andrew Yellen, PhD, and Thomas Schweller, MD, a board-certified neurologist and professor of neurology at the University of California, San Diego, have closely examined the effects of light sensitivity and Irlen Syndrome utilizing state-of-the-art Visual Evoked Responses (VER) called DESAR. The objective neuroelectrical evidence from their 2009 study showed abnormal visual activity or a delay in visual processing for those who have Irlen Syndrome.[1]

According to their study, the brain is constantly receiving visual information. However, for those with Irlen Syndrome, instead of easily processing the signals, the brain is stunned and has no time to recover before receiving more information. This is much like the effect of looking at continuous flashbulbs going off. It is believed that the overlapping information is responsible for the distortions associated with Irlen Syndrome. Yellen and Schweller concluded that people with Irlen Syndrome have difficulty filtering and processing visual information in the brain.

Another study, conducted at the Center for Advanced Medical Technologies at the University of Utah's School of Medicine, used another type of brain scan, a MEG. This study yielded similar results, showing that those with Irlen Syndrome had difficulty processing visual information. In addition, the study presented objective evidence establishing not just the presence of a problem, but also that the issue can be corrected by Irlen Filters. The MEG scans showed the normal processing of visual information with Irlen Filters.

The results of the brain having to work harder to process visual information can also be seen with studies from Amen Clinics using a SPECT (single photon emission computed tomography) scan. When Dr. Amen compared the brain scans of 42 people with Irlen Syndrome to those of 200 people with no evidence of Irlen Syndrome, he found:

> There are areas of increased activity in the brain's emotional and visual processing centers and decreased activity in the cerebellum, an area that helps to integrate coordination and new information [for people] with Irlen Syndrome. In performing scans after using Irlen Filters as the only intervention, we have seen the brain become significantly more balanced. I have often been amazed at the improvements our patients have experienced. A calmer brain is better able to correctly process visual information.[2]
>
> Irlen Syndrome is largely about the effects of light on the brain. Remarkably, when people obtain benefit from the treatment, it helps to balance brain function. One of the factors that drew me to [Irlen Syndrome] and the Irlen treatment is its simplicity and effectiveness.[3]

Figures 7.1 and 7.2 show brain scans that were taken using SPECT technology. Both figures show the portions of the brain that are in heavy use, or "hot." The same brain was used for both scans. However, Figure 7.1 was taken when the person was not wearing Irlen Filters, and Figure 7.2 was taken after Irlen Filters were being worn. As you can see, there are many more "hot" areas of the brain in Figure 7.1—and in Figure 7.2, brain usage has decreased significantly to a much more "normalized" level.

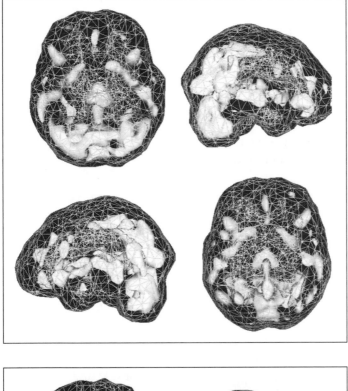

Figure 7.1.
SPECT Scan
Without Irlen
Filters.
Without Irlen
Filters, many
more areas of
the brain are
being heavily
used.

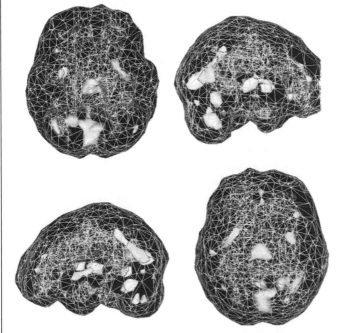

Figure 7.2.
SPECT Scan
With Irlen
Filters.
With Irlen Filters,
brain usage
decreases
to a more
normalized
amount.

CONCLUSION

You don't need to have Irlen Syndrome to suffer from light sensitivity. Even if someone does not have Irlen Syndrome, light sensitivity issues and its associated symptoms can be vastly improved with the aid of Irlen Filters. Just as hundreds of thousands of people have come to Irlen Clinics worldwide to stop words from moving around on the printed page, my hope now is that individuals who struggle with light sensitivity will also choose to contact an Irlen Diagnostician. This very real problem affects people worldwide and is a major cause of stress that most often goes unnoticed.

Your brain is constantly processing visual information. The information is not sent to the brain as a picture, but rather is converted in wavelengths of light or colors. For those with Irlen symptoms, the brain has difficulty processing certain colors or wavelengths of light. Thus, the brain is working harder than it should. Brain imaging studies of individuals with Irlen Syndrome have provided a clearer picture of why lighting, reading, fluorescent colors, patterns, and other visual activities create fatigue, chronic stress, distortions, and physical symptoms.

Brain studies have led to an understanding of the neurological differences between individuals with Irlen symptoms—whether inherited or acquired—and individuals who do not have these difficulties. This new technology of brain imaging allows neuroscientists to pinpoint which parts of the brain become over-activated and which parts calm down when the individual is wearing Irlen Spectral Filters. This shows how the filtering of specific wavelengths of light or color can be used to calm the brain so it can function properly. In other words, these brain scans help prove that the Irlen Method is effective.

In the next chapter, we will explore some of the other issues that can be helped significantly by wearing Irlen Filters, with an emphasis on headaches and migraines.

8

Headaches, Migraines, and Irlen Syndrome

When Gregory first came to see us, he was nine years old. A straight-A student, Gregory suffered from daily headaches and stomachaches and felt sick whenever he was in school. By the end of the semester, his mother was frequently being called by the school nurse to come pick him up.

Gregory's parents knew that he was not fabricating his symptoms, even though none could be attributed to either a visual or medical problem. He never liked reading, and when he did read, it took a lot out of him. After ten to fifteen minutes, he would complain of headaches and would stop. If he read any longer, he would feel dizzy and sick to his stomach.

He also reported that the white pages seemed as bright as looking into the sun. It wasn't just reading that triggered symptoms for Gregory, but fluorescent lights and whiteboards as well.

Today, Gregory is wearing his Irlen Filters and no longer reports these daily physical symptoms.

—GREGORY, IRLEN CLIENT FILES

During our many years of working with individuals with Irlen Syndrome and Irlen-like symptoms, we have been able to help numerous people who frequently suffer from headaches and migraines. Headaches and migraines can have one or more triggers. In this chapter, we hope to open your eyes to all the triggers that can be eliminated by the Irlen Method. Too many people are needlessly suffering in silence. It does not have to be that way.

MISUNDERSTOOD, MISDIAGNOSED, AND MISTREATED

Nearly 18 million Americans report regular headaches to doctors and medical professionals, but only about half of those people are being treated. As a group, headache sufferers are probably the most misunderstood, misdiagnosed, and mistreated patients in modern medicine.

There are a variety of reasons why someone may get headaches, including medical conditions, reactions to medication, reactions to food, the result of a visual problem, or—as we have discovered—a side effect of lighting and visual-perceptual activities. When the triggers for headaches are lighting and/or reading, the ramifications are enormous, pervasive, and will only increase as the student moves up in school. As the academic demands increase and more reading is required, headaches can—and often do—become more pronounced, severe, and frequent. What first start out as headaches can become migraines. You may be wondering why children don't tell their parents or teachers when their head hurts. In some cases, they do not know that this is abnormal and that they should tell someone. However, some of the time, their headaches have been dismissed because there is no visual or medical condition. Instead, students should be encouraged to report headaches, and such reports should not be taken lightly.

Misunderstood

About 60 percent of all children suffer occasional headaches, according to the National Headache Foundation. This is an alarming statistic. However, most of the time, families do not take their children's headaches seriously, especially if no medical or visual reason can be identified. Teachers, as well as parents, often assume that the child who complains is simply trying to get out of doing schoolwork, homework, or chores. In reality, these children may not be able to perform in class because of headaches or the other physical symptoms that accompany them, such as nausea or dizziness. These children are often seen sitting with their heads down, not being able to pay attention or simply not listening to the teacher. Many times when we do not believe a child or take her seriously, she will simply stop reporting headaches. However, the symptoms do not go away.

Misdiagnosed: Help Is on the Way

To make matters worse, when such physical symptoms are the underlying problem and have not been identified, students are often mislabeled with terms such as ADD, ADHD, learning disabilities, depression, or even dyslexia. Too often, teachers and guidance counselors throw labels on children rather than asking the often ignored but important questions about how the child feels physically. Then, when a child says that she has a headache or feels nauseous, it is typically chalked up to the fact that she is tired, stressed, or has the infamous "bug" that always seems to be going around schools. The connection is rarely ever made between the physical environment—such as lighting, reading, or working on the computer—and the physical symptoms. However, these symptoms are real and should not be ignored.

There is a tendency to think that if a student is doing well in school, she is not struggling with headaches. However, many children who are highly motivated will endure headaches, fatigue, or a variety of other symptoms in order to succeed in school. I have spoken with many adults who enjoy reading, but pay the price by living with headaches. In fact, I recall seeing a law student who refused to believe he had a problem. When his sister, whose grades went from Cs to As in college after she started wearing Irlen Filters, told him to try the Irlen Method, his rebuttal was that he was in law school and obviously didn't have a problem. To make a long story short, he finally realized that the physical symptoms he was suffering from were limiting his performance when he failed to pass the bar exam three times. He would become tired and sleepy very quickly while studying, forcing him to stop. He would drink coffee non-stop. When he took the bar exams, he could not read them all the way through without his eyes hurting, feeling exhausted, and having a headache. The bottom line is that some students will just assume that because they are working hard, headaches come with the territory. This is typically not the case.

Mistreated

Naturally, a misdiagnosis can—and often does—lead to mistreatment. There are so many different triggers for headaches that it is often difficult to identify the underlying causes. When light sensitivity is ignored as a trigger there can be a variety of different scenarios. Headaches can become migraines and medication prescribed not only doesn't eliminate the migraines, but can have side effects. Individuals who live with headaches may keep their heads down on the desk, spend time in their dark bedrooms, or sleep a lot. These behaviors can lead to a misdiagnosis of depression, resulting in medication that is not effective. Usually the misdiagnosis is stress for mistreatment—which is, much of the time, no treatment at all. It is absolutely essential to identify the underlying cause and treat it. The wrong help will not only be a waste of time but also means the sufferer has to continue living with headaches or migraines.

THE ROOT OF THE PROBLEM

There are many different reasons why people—children and adults—may suffer from headaches or migraines. In many instances, headaches and migraines stem from visual and medical problems, which require medical attention.

A child or adult complaining of regular headaches should start looking for answers by first seeing an eye or medical doctor. In some cases, the solution may be as simple as a need for glasses or a stronger optical prescription. In other cases, thyroid conditions, sinuses, or even allergies may be the culprit.

However, approximately 75 percent of headaches have no known cause and are described as tension headaches related to stress. For these headaches, treatment is difficult. Usually, the individual is left to try over-the-counter medications or alternative treatments and therapies like biofeedback, stress management, yoga, chiropractic adjustments, hypnosis, or aromatherapy. However, the answer may be as simple as wearing Irlen Filters.

Since there can be numerous causes for headaches, it is important to identify and address all of the triggers. The list below gives some of the most common triggers. These are described in greater detail—along with other possible causes and accommodations—in Appendix A (see page 176).

- Eating Patterns. Some individuals must eat small meals on a frequent basis or they will feel sick and/or get headaches. Adults often wait until they have a headache before eating, and children often cannot eat as frequently as necessary due to their school schedules. Some children may need special permission to eat snacks at school if they cannot wait until their lunch period or the end of the school day without getting a headache or feeling sick.

- Food Sensitivity. A variety of different foods can trigger headaches. Some of the more commonly reported food triggers are sugar, chocolate, cheese, red wine, yeast, dairy products, wheat, MSG, preservatives, additives, and food dyes.

- Lighting, glare, reading, and visual activities can also trigger headaches and migraines. The rest of this chapter will explore these triggers in greater detail, and also identify the solution.

- Smells. Strong smells, such as perfumes, soaps, sprays, hand lotions, hair sprays, colognes, glues, and dry erase markers can trigger headaches, stomachaches, and dizziness.

If medical or visual problems are not the root cause of the headaches, or if the headaches or physical symptoms persist even after treatment for a medical or visual problem, the root may be a perceptual problem such as Irlen Syndrome. Unfortunately, too many people stop looking for answers once the doctor and/or optometrist gives them a clean bill of health, making the assumption that if the pain doesn't go away on its own, they will just have to get used to living with it.

Other Red Flags

To find out if you should consider the Irlen Method, you can look for what I call "red flags" which may indicate that your child is experiencing headaches and not saying anything. These red flags are non-verbal behaviors that indicate something may be wrong. For example, you may want to be aware if your child is doing anything on the following list.

Your child may be suffering from headaches if she:

- Blinks a lot while reading or blinks a lot in general

- Constantly changes position while reading

- Looks up or away from the page often

- Moves back and forth while reading

- Moves closer to the page

- Rubs her eyes often

- Squints to read or squints in general

- Stops reading to take frequent breaks

If your child frequently displays one or more of the behaviors on the list, it is a signal that she may be experiencing strain and fatigue, both of which can lead to headaches and other physical symptoms that can be eliminated with Irlen Spectral Filters. Displaying some of the behaviors on the list may also indicate that she is already experiencing headaches.

Of course, you cannot always tell if your child has a headache by observing, so you also have to ask questions. When your child wants to stop reading, that's when you should ask the following questions: How do you feel? How does your head feel? How does your stomach feel? Sometimes the physical symptoms are manifested as feeling tired or dizzy. Find out what your child is experiencing.

It is important to remember that these red flags do not pertain to only reading from the page but also include writing, copying, doing math problems, reading music, or working on a computer screen. If Irlen is the problem, any activity that requires visual perception can be at the root of the problem. Lighting, whiteboards, overhead projectors, power point presentations, watching videos or television, playing video games, or even something as simple as looking at wallpaper can trigger the red flags.

Additionally, glare can cause discomfort. It may often be the result of a reflection of light from the sun or a man-made source. Glare can be as simple as the sunlight bouncing off of a shiny car or perhaps from street-lights in the dark night. Often the contrast of the brightness of the light in otherwise darker conditions makes the glare more disturbing to some-one who is light sensitive.

Since everyone's brain is different, the triggers for those with Irlen may not be exactly the same, or as pronounced, as they are for someone else; but the ones that are mentioned above can be eliminated by wearing Irlen Spectral Filters.

HEADACHES AND OTHER ACTIVITIES

While there is a clear connection between reading and headaches, there is not always an obvious connection made between headaches and other visual activities. Remember, visual perception includes much more than simply reading words off a printed page. Headaches and other symptoms can occur during other visual activities as well. (To determine if the Irlen method can help your headaches, see the test on pages 112 and 113.)

Computer Work

The combination of bright backlighting, movement, color, letters, words, numbers, and graphics can easily illustrate why computers can be another trigger for stress and subsequent physical symptoms, especially for anyone with light sensitivity issues.

Copying

Copying combines the components of both reading and writing, both of which can cause the same physical strain that leads to headaches or other physical symptoms.

Driving

Driving requires that you pay attention to movement and visual stimuli constantly coming from all sides. The movement, glare, and colors add levels of stress as the driver is looking and trying to process information quickly, which can be a trigger for headaches, migraines, and other physical symptoms.

Night driving adds another component: lights. For people with light sensitivity, the added lights at night make it that much harder to drive. Headlights, brake lights, streetlights, and glare are all potential stressors. These are in addition to the fast processing of information that is required to drive.

Math

I have asked children if they wear their Irlen Filters when they are doing math, and they almost always say, "No, it's not reading, it's math." Children often do not associate the fact that when they are processing numbers off of a page, it is a form of reading. Numbers and mathematical symbols can have the same effect on a person as reading words and letters. In order to do math problems, the numbers must stay in their columns and you must be able to read small symbols, which can be difficult for someone with Irlen Syndrome. Headaches and physical symptoms resulting from math problems are not at all uncommon.

Movies or Television

Both movies and television present an array of fast movement and color, which can be stressful for the brain to process and can lead to physical symptoms, including headaches.

Patterns and Colors

Visual patterns can also be triggers for headaches and other physical symptoms. Looking at patterned wallpaper and doing a needlepoint activity are both classified as patterns. Most people who have Irlen Syndrome consider white as being bright, but there are other colors, especially fluorescent colors, that can be stress triggers. Stripes and polka-dots are patterns that can be most difficult.

Writing

Very often people do not associate writing with reading. However, you don't write without looking at the words and reading them as you proceed across the page. Reading, re-reading, and re-writing are all important components of being able to write in an organized fashion. Therefore, you can't ignore the fact that reading goes hand in hand with writing and can also yield a physical reaction.

The result of these activities and other environmental factors is stress, which can change the brain and, subsequently, change how a person feels, acts, and performs. What these activities have in common is that they all require visual processing and, in most cases, the need to process information quickly. For people with Irlen Syndrome, this is difficult. The added stress from attempting any of these activities can, and often does, result in headaches or migraines.

MIGRAINES

In the United States, it is estimated that 24 million people are affected by migraines each year—roughly 17 percent of women and 6 percent of men. Migraines are extremely painful headaches that can be accompanied by a variety of symptoms, such as dizziness, nausea, and even hallucinations. According to the National Headache Foundation, migraines and other headaches account for about 157 million lost working days in a year. The end result indicates that the social, physical, and economic results of migraines are significant. At present, there is no definitive cure for a migraine.

For many years, conventional medicine hasn't had much to offer migraine sufferers. The usual solution has been to reach for aspirin, pain relief, or prescription medication and then lie down in a dark, quiet room and wait for the pain to subside. Attempting sleep has also been suggested to help.

Triggers of migraine headaches are highly individualized. Literature on migraines suggest that foods such as wheat, cheese, and chocolate as well as food additives, alcohol (most commonly red wine), caffeine, certain medications, and stress are all triggers of migraines. Light is mentioned as a trigger but is often overlooked. Migraines may also be the result of visual-perceptual problems as well, such as those caused by environmental factors (like lighting and of the ones listed above). In these cases, migraines can be avoided or alleviated by wearing Irlen Filters.

LIVING WITH HEADACHES OR MIGRAINES

Headaches have become a part of life for far too many individuals. Some headache sufferers have become adept at differentiating between the different types of headaches they get. For example, some people know that they can eliminate certain headaches caused by the environment by wearing Irlen Filters, while another headache will be the result of a different source, such as a strong smell or food sensitivity. These types of headaches can't be eliminated by using Irlen Filters—only headaches triggered by lighting, reading, and the other visual activities mentioned above can be. Individuals learn to differentiate between different types of headaches based on how the headache first surfaces and where they first feel the pain. Headaches take many forms and can start in the temple, forehead, back of the head, or even behind the eyes. Some people are aware of the different sources that cause their headaches. This is something anyone can learn to do.

Again, it is very important not to ignore headaches or assume there is no solution. The buildup of stress and the agony of living with headaches can take its toll on your quality of life.

When headaches go unreported or untreated because the cause is not identified, the sufferer pays a price. For example, if a student is living with headaches and/or other physical symptoms, it affects many aspects of her life, particularly academic performance. It is hard to think, concentrate, and work when your head hurts. It is very difficult to read or do other academic tasks when you know doing so will only cause you to experience pain.

Allowing Headaches to Change Your Life

My daughter had headaches on a daily basis for most of her life. Searching for answers was a frustrating and painful journey. Along with headaches, she suffered from migraines, dizziness, loss of appetite, and learning difficulties. When she would come home from school, she would close herself in her bedroom with the lights off and the shades down. We took her to see an MD, a neurologist, a head and neck specialist, an optometrist, and a physical therapist. Neither an MRI nor a blood test showed anything unusual. Doctors told her that her headaches were caused by tension and stress, and they continued to prescribe medications for the pain.

Irlen Self-Test for Headaches, Migraines, Stress, or Strain

To see if headaches can be eliminated by the Irlen Method, you need to determine if any of the items or activities on the following list bother your or your child's eyes, head, or stomach or create feelings of dizziness, tiredness, nervousness, anxiety, or irritability.

- Bright lights

- Bright or neon colors

- Certain patterns or stripes

- Doing visually-intensive activities like needlepoint, cross-stitching, woodworking, or crossword puzzles

- Glare off high-gloss white paper

- Glare off the chrome on cars

- Glare on hazy days

- Headlights from oncoming traffic

- Reading black print on high-gloss white paper

- Reading textbooks

- Sunlight

Finally, my daughter discovered the Irlen Method. She was tested, diagnosed, and fitted for Irlen Filters. By wearing her Irlen Filters, she can now read, write, copy, and do her homework pain-free. It was a great relief to discover what she was suffering from and to learn that there was something she could do about it.

—HEIDI, IRLEN CLIENT FILES

In your attempt to avoid headaches, you can certainly alter your lifestyle. It is not ideal, but it can be easy to avoid red wine or a particular food if these have been identified as triggers for your headaches or migraines. However, it is very difficult—if not impossible—to avoid reading, writing, or fluorescent lighting. If reading, writing, fluorescent lighting, or

---

- Working on the computer

- Working or reading under fluorescent lights

Once you have determined which activities and situations make you or your child feel ill, ask the following questions.

Circle the answer that best describes your situation.

- Do I feel antsy or fidgety when under fluorescent lighting?   Yes   No

- Do I feel like there is not enough light when reading?   Yes   No

- Do I feel like there is too much light when reading?   Yes   No

- Do I get a headache from fluorescent lighting?   Yes   No

- Do I usually read in dim lighting?   Yes   No

- Does my performance deteriorate under bright or fluorescent lighting?   Yes   No

If one or more of the items on the first part of the list make you or your child feel ill, and if the answer was "yes" to three of more of the questions above, this indicates that lighting, glare, and/or visual activities are triggers for headaches, migraines, or other symptoms you or your child may be experiencing. The higher the score, the more lighting and/or visually-intensive activities are contributing to the pain.

the variety of other visual activities mentioned in this chapter is what is triggering your headaches, these triggers are more difficult to avoid, and you need to consider the Irlen Method.

Perhaps the most extreme case I've seen was the girl who started having headaches in first grade. By sixth grade, in addition to having almost daily headaches, she felt dizzy, sick to her stomach, and had migraines. She tried hard to do her schoolwork, but reading made her feel even sicker. She tried over-the-counter pills and various medications, none of which helped. When she was in high school, she overdosed on prescription medication. She didn't want to kill herself; she just wanted so badly to stop the pain. She was rushed to the hospital where she was treated. However, she had other labels placed on her, such as "depressed" and "suicidal." Soon she was getting outside therapy, but still her headaches and migraines continued. It was fortunate for the girl that her school psychologist, whom she was strongly recommended to see, also happened to be an Irlen Screener who asked her questions that no one else had ever asked. The screener asked the girl how she felt in class under the fluorescent lights and how she felt when she read, wrote, or worked on the computer. To each question she answered, "Sick." Her responses allowed the Irlen Screener to identify the cause of her headaches and subsequently get her the help she needed.

Our success with the Irlen Method in eliminating physical symptoms, including headaches and migraines, is significant. If the headaches are caused by light sensitivity and/or visual activities (with no other contributing factors), the Irlen Method can eliminate all or almost all of the sufferer's symptoms.

Medication

Many people try taking over-the-counter medications to alleviate their headaches. Such medications can mask the pain temporarily but are not very effective in eliminating pain in the long-term. Medications for migraines are also typically strong and can have their own negative side effects. Patients list sleepiness and fatigue, racing heartbeat, nausea, and difficulty thinking as common side effects. Other less frequently mentioned side effects included dizziness, muscle weakness, chest pressure, and warm sensations. People often find that they get used to the medication and have to take more and more to get any benefit. Even then, medications can be useful but are not actually solving the problem, serving instead as a stopgap.

CONCLUSION

I thought it would be appropriate to conclude this chapter by mentioning some interesting research. A study was conducted at the University of Birmingham in England. The study illustrated that many migraine sufferers are sensitive to the flickering from fluorescent lighting, TV screens, and computer monitors. The study found that wearing colored lenses reduced the frequency of migraine headaches by 74 percent.

Other research studies indicate that about one in five individuals get relief from headaches and migraines by wearing colored glasses. A preliminary study conducted at the University of Texas Medical School at Houston focused attention on thirty migraine sufferers and found that twenty-seven of them, or 90 percent, were helped dramatically by colored contact lenses.

Finally, an unpublished study conducted in the United Kingdom that looked at a group of migraine sufferers who had been wearing Irlen Filters for six months to five years found that for 83 percent of the people in the study, the filters reduced both the frequency and the severity of their migraines.

Headaches and migraines are very real problems, often misdiagnosed, misunderstood, and mistreated. Numerous triggers are the culprit, especially today with so much around us to stimulate our senses. Unfortunately, too many people have become accustomed to living with headaches. We have found, as noted in this chapter, that both headaches and more painful, intrusive migraines can benefit from Irlen Filters.

In the next chapter we explore the world of attention deficit disorders. This condition can also be misunderstood, misdiagnosed, and mistreated. In many cases, what is thought to be ADD or ADHD is actually Irlen Syndrome.

9

Attention Deficit Disorders and Irlen Syndrome

Over many years I have consulted with parents who have concerns about their children's attention span and learning abilities. Many of the children in question had already been diagnosed with attention deficit disorder. After meeting with these children, I suggested that many of them be evaluated for Irlen Syndrome.

It has been amazing to me how many of these children—when diagnosed with and treated for Irlen Syndrome—no longer met the criteria for ADD. The Irlen Method has been a powerful and exciting tool for children and often for their parents as well.

—FAY VAN DER KAR LEVINSON, PhD, MEMBER OF APA AND A
LICENSED PSYCHOLOGIST IN PRIVATE PRACTICE FOR THIRTY YEARS

If you spend any time around schools today, you will inevitably hear the term "attention deficit disorder." The number of children diagnosed with attention problems has reached epidemic proportions. In fact, it is estimated that three to five percent of school-age children in the United States (or roughly two million children) have been diagnosed with an attention deficit disorder (ADD or ADHD). It is estimated that almost half of the children who have these issues will continue to exhibit symptoms as adults. However, as you will learn in this chapter, many times children are diagnosed with attention deficit disorder, with or without hyperactivity, when the issue is actually Irlen Syndrome. (See the inset on pages 120 and 121.) When these children are properly treated, their symptoms go away.

ADD AND ADHD

Many people wonder what the difference between ADD and ADHD is. Essentially, ADD refers to an attention problem only, while ADHD refers to an attention problem with hyperactivity and impulsivity. Symptoms of ADD and ADHD are similar to those of Irlen Syndrome, and this is why diagnosis can be confusing.

In order to understand the relationship between these two types of attention deficit disorder and Irlen Syndrome, it is not necessary to talk about them as separate entities. Therefore, to simplify discussions in this chapter and for the rest of the book, all references to ADD and ADHD from this point on will be referred to as simply "AD/HD."

Difficulties of Diagnosing AD/HD

AD/HD has a strong neurological basis, and the precise cause has not yet been identified. The main symptoms are limited or poor attention span, an inability to focus, and distractibility; but those labeled AD/HD also have impulsive or hyper behavior. These symptoms cause concern because they can lead to poor performance in school or at work, poor social skills and relationships, and low self-esteem. It is often difficult for people with AD/HD to master time management and organizational skills. Tasks such as planning and finishing assignments, organizing events or activities, following and participating in conversations, and maintaining relationships can be difficult.

Even though AD/HD can only be treated by a medical doctor, there are presently no medical tests to diagnose the disorder. Diagnosis is most often based on parents and teachers completing a checklist of behaviors associated with AD/HD. Even when used in conjunction with other information, such as developmental history and school records, the diagnosis remains subjective and can, therefore, be misleading.

Even the less subjective computerized method of diagnosing AD/HD, where the individual sits in front of a computer screen while completing a variety of visually-intensive (and purposely tedious and/or boring) activities, can be misleading. Those with Irlen Syndrome have difficulty maintaining focus on a computer screen for any length of time. This can lead to people with Irlen Syndrome being misdiagnosed with attention deficit disorder.

Difficulties

Coming up with an accurate diagnosis can be difficult for a number of reasons. Identification methods are, as mentioned, subjective. For example, the teacher may notice that the child puts his head down on the desk or simply does not do his class work. The parents may be told by a teacher that their child is inattentive or distracted in class, and testing may be recommended. While these behaviors can certainly be attributed to AD/HD, there are a number of other issues that can cause similar behaviors—including Irlen Syndrome.

Generally, people hope there is a one-to-one correlation between symptoms and a diagnosis, which is true for most medical conditions. Typically, there is a group of symptoms indicating a specific problem, which leads to a medical diagnosis usually identified through medical testing and subsequently treated by medication. The problem with AD/HD is that the behaviors can also be related to many different causes. For example, other medical problems, dietary sensitivities, undetected visual or hearing problems, undetected reading and learning difficulties, sensory sensitivities, and even emotional problems can yield behaviors similar to those associated with AD/HD. Some parents report that sugar makes their child antsy, fidgety, or overactive. Gluten and casein (a protein found in milk and used independently in many foods as a binding agent) have also been shown to result in similar behaviors. The same can be true of food additives, food dyes, and even allergic reactions.

Therefore, many individuals are mistakenly diagnosed as having AD/HD and are unnecessarily medicated when a more practical non-medical intervention is available. Fortunately, I think most parents today are becoming aware that behavioral issues do not automatically translate to AD/HD. Parents should not immediately jump to medication as the answer without first considering all of the other possible root causes. Think of these behaviors as being on the top floor of a building. To find out what is causing these behaviors, you need to explore all of the other floors of the building. As a parent, you need to open up the doors and look inside. See Appendix A (page 176) to help identify some of the possible undetected causes of these behaviors. As with any problem, one or more issues may need to be addressed before behavior improves.

Pros and Cons of Medication

Knowing the cause of a problem is essential when seeking the right treatment. The medications can be very positive and life-changing—for children who actually have AD/HD. However, research indicates that nearly

Irlen, the Root Cause of a Misdiagnosis

The behaviors associated with Irlen Syndrome are also very similar to AD/HD-related behaviors. Individuals who have AD/HD and those who have Irlen Syndrome find that the longer and harder they try, the worse it gets. It would be like riding a bike and peddling harder but going slower. The difference is that when the problem is Irlen Syndrome, distractibility and inattentiveness often occur while reading, writing, working on the computer, or even sitting and listening to a lecture while under fluorescent lights. Someone with Irlen Syndrome may look away from a whiteboard or put his head down on the desk due to a headache or other physical symptoms. The same behavior may result when a child views letters on the page moving around when reading. To the teacher, this will look like an unwillingness to focus. However, for someone with Irlen Syndrome, this is not the case.

It is important to understand how for someone with Irlen Syndrome, certain environmental stimuli can cause behaviors that could be misdiagnosed as AD/HD. For this reason, I include the following two scenarios, one caused by lighting and the other caused by reading difficulties. For someone with Irlen Syndrome, reading, other academic tasks, and lighting—especially fluorescent lighting—can create behaviors similar to AD/HD.

Lighting

Pretend that you have to spend every afternoon for a week in a room where the lights are constantly flickering on and off. Of course, you would find it annoying, and you would likely want to leave. But what if you couldn't leave? You would soon become over-stimulated to the point of distraction. Not only would it be difficult on your eyes, but listening to a lecture, paying attention, or completing an assignment would also be extremely trying. You would likely find yourself feeling irritable or anxious. As a result, you might put your head down and close your eyes.

Due to your behavior, you would appear to be someone who is inattentive and unable to sit still. Someone observing your behavior might very easily conclude that you could have AD/HD. Hence, based on your behaviors, you could theoretically be misdiagnosed with AD/HD rather than properly diagnosed with Irlen Syndrome.

one-third of the children on these medications have been misdiagnosed. That means that nearly one-third of children are being wrongfully medicated and can experience worrisome side effects including decreased appetite, weight loss, insomnia, abdominal pain, and personality changes. Other less common side effects can include increasing anxiety, irritability, involuntary tick activity (such as eye blinking and facial grimaces), cough-

In the fourth grade, my grandson was diagnosed with AD/HD and placed on medication. He got weepy for no reason and couldn't sleep. He tried various medications, all with negative side effects. On one medication he got lethargic; on another he couldn't eat or sleep. I just remember thinking, "This isn't right." We finally realized that his problems only occurred during school when he was under fluorescent lighting. It was a revelation to see the difference that lighting made to his behavior and attitude.

—BRENDA, IRLEN CLIENT FILES

Reading

Think about what it would be like to read a book while sitting on a vibrating chair. It would likely be frustrating, but you may be able to complete the task. Now, imagine that the words in the book you are reading are printed on clear plastic, and someone is shining a very bright light directly into your eyes from behind the plastic. Combine the light with the vibrating chair and imagine what reading under those conditions would be like. You would not want to look at the page. You would not be able to keep looking at the page without suffering headaches, nausea, or other symptoms. If you knew ahead of time that this is what reading would feel like, you would not want to start such a painful and frustrating task. As you kept trying to read or do your work, the jiggling letters and numbers would start to swirl and disappear. As a result, you would keep looking up or perhaps even get up to look out the window. You might find yourself daydreaming instead of doing your work.

For some children with Irlen Syndrome, such distortions make them feel fidgety and anxious. These children will constantly move, talk to classmates, or do anything they can think of besides their work. If someone were constantly getting up, walking around, or disturbing other children when they should be working, the teacher would probably not understand how difficult and painful it was for that person to look at printed words, letters, and numbers. A teacher in this situation would most likely believe that the student had AD/HD.

ing, or throat clearing. These reactions may then lead physicians to prescribe additional medications to control the negative side effects.

Most physicians in the United States prescribe medications for AD/HD based on their own personal preference since there is no objective blood test or other means of determining the correct medication, combination of medications, or dosage. Often, a trial-and-error approach starts with one medication being prescribed and then switches to another and another until one is found that produces the desired results. This can be very difficult for the child.

Controversy

Diagnoses of attention deficit disorders continue to increase. Some may say it is a trend, or the "flavor of the week," when it comes to finding a reason why a child is not performing well in school. Many teachers seek fast and easy solutions in an attempt to better control classroom behavior and increase academic performance, which is why a lot of teachers are quick to push for a diagnosis and medication. They want children who sit still, do not disturb others, do their work without supervision, and pay attention. While these are admirable goals, medication is not always the way to achieve such results.

WATCHING THE BEHAVIORS

While many teachers are quick to label a child as likely having AD/HD, more and more parents are looking to try alternative approaches. To do this, parents should start by using their own observations.

The typical behaviors that are associated with both Irlen Syndrome and AD/HD may include fatigue, distractibility, daydreaming, and becoming easily frustrated. Additional symptoms may include a need for frequent movement or a change of activity, difficulty sitting still, and difficulty following through and completing tasks. As mentioned before, these behaviors can have many different causes, all of which can be mistaken for AD/HD.

Does Your Child Have Irlen Syndrome?

To determine if your child may have Irlen Syndrome rather than AD/HD, you might ask yourself the following questions.

Does your child:

- Fidget or squirm only in school or while reading (or doing homework) but not at other times such as while watching television or playing a game?

- Get easily distracted, but not in play situations?

- Have difficulty following through with academic work?

- Have difficulty sitting still and concentrating in class, but not when the activity is enjoyable?

- Seem to be in constant motion in class under the fluorescent lights but not at home?

If you answered "yes" to more than one of these questions, you should seek Irlen testing for a diagnosis and treatment.

Consistency of Behavior

When making observations about your child's behavior, it is important to look for consistency. One critical difference between Irlen Syndrome and an attention deficit disorder is the consistency of the behavior. A child with AD/HD will display symptoms not only in school, but also at home and elsewhere. Often, the parents who resist medicating their child are usually the ones who see a different child at home than the one the teacher reports seeing in class. "The school is telling me that my child can't sit still, bothers other children, and is inattentive," explained one concerned mom who came to see me. "But I don't see the same thing at home. This is not the child I see around the house."

As detectives watching our children's behaviors, we need to look at whether or not the behavior occurs only at school, only at home, or in all situations. Is it related to academic activities like homework or schoolwork? Does it occur only when the child is reading? Does he become inattentive only under bright lights? If the behavior is inconsistent, occurring only in certain situations, it is more likely to be related to Irlen Syndrome than AD/HD. On the contrary, if a parent sees his child having trouble staying focused in *all* situations—in school, at home, sitting down at the dinner table to eat, or playing games—then the culprit is more likely AD/HD. With AD/HD, it doesn't matter whether the child enjoys the activity or not. Whether at play or at work, he will display the same type(s) of behavior.

One of my favorite examples of an individual with AD/HD comes from one of the greatest inventors in American history—Thomas Edison. Edison had a long table at which he would typically work on several inventions at one time. To do this, he would sit on a chair with rollers. He would work on one invention for a few minutes, roll over to another invention and work on that one, and a few minutes later, he would roll over to another.[1]

My favorite example of a child misdiagnosed is Becky.

Since her kindergarten year, my husband and I have been searching for answers to our daughter Becky's learning challenges. We checked her vision, which was 20/20. We tried a summer reading workshop. She hated it. She went to an eye therapy program that was "guaranteed" success. It didn't work.

Becky's teacher recommended she be tested for AD/HD. So we had her tested. The diagnosis was, in fact, AD/HD, and medication was prescribed. However, we saw no improvement. Through her third and fourth grade years, we waited for her to grow out of it, even though we weren't entirely sure what "it" was. It was an extremely frustrating time—everything we tried seemed to only exacerbate the issues.

As it turned out, Becky had Irlen Syndrome. Since we did not know how she saw the world, we had never gotten her appropriate help. She never told us that the words scrolled toward her like the Star Wars *movie credits, flashed at her like a lightening storm, blurred like a jittering earthquake, and flowed like a river. How could she know that words were supposed to stay in one place? As a result, Becky appeared inattentive when, in reality, reading a page was exasperating for her.*

All of Becky's symptoms vanished once she put on her Irlen Filters.

—BECKY, IRLEN CLIENT FILES

Heredity

Since Irlen Syndrome is inherited, one thing parents can do is to try some personal experimentation. For example, you can compare and see if there is a difference in how you feel in dim lighting versus how you feel in fluorescent lighting. After a while, does the lighting bother you? Do you experience a headache or start to feel fidgety or nervous? Doing a self-assessment may provide you with clues about your child. Your symptoms may be the same as those your child is experiencing in school. Understanding how you feel can help you understand how your child feels and can prove very beneficial when it comes to making a proper diagnosis.

Overlaps or More Than One Issue

One of the reasons that reactions to food, allergies, reading problems, and other undetected issues are mentioned in this chapter is that there can be an overlap between these issues and AD/HD or Irlen Syndrome. Some people who have AD/HD also have Irlen Syndrome. Other people may have food sensitivities and also have Irlen Syndrome or AD/HD. Irlen Spectral Filters can take away only the behaviors associated with

Irlen Syndrome. However, there may still be other factors involved that are contributing to the child's behavior. It is then important to look at the remaining problems and address them as well.

You always want to go step by step, layer by layer, and ask yourself what you are missing. As a parent—and a detective—you need to consider every possibility that may be contributing to your child's behavior. Try hard not to think that only one problem can be causing your child's difficulties. For example, AD/HD may be causing attention problems while, at the same time, Irlen Syndrome and/or smell sensitivities may be causing headaches or irritability. Additionally, remember the importance of only trying one intervention at a time to help your child (see below).

BRAIN FUNCTIONS

Neuroimaging studies of the brains of individuals with attention deficit disorder show excessive or slow brainwave activity in areas of the brain associated with learning, memory, self-control, decision making, and the ability to pay attention, focus on tasks, and concentrate. Over-arousal of certain areas is associated with hyperactivity.

Interestingly, the brain studies of individuals with Irlen Syndrome indicate similar brain activity. In addition to the visual cortex being over-stimulated and not being able to process visual information well, the cortex can show the same pattern of over- or under-activity for those with Irlen Syndrome, thus creating the same behavioral problems that are seen in patients with AD/HD.

REAL LIFE STORIES: TELLING IT MY WAY

The following vignettes are about Irlen clients who were misdiagnosed with attention deficit disorder. I present their stories in an attempt to reframe how people look at behaviors. Keep in mind that behaviors do not tell the whole story, and misdiagnosis can lead to years of frustration.

One at a Time

If you are going to try different interventions to help your child, make sure you only try one at a time. Otherwise, it is difficult to know which intervention is creating positive results. Remember, your child may need a combination of different treatments in order to improve. Only make one change at a time so that you can see the individual results.

Distraction

Joseph knew he had problems in school. He couldn't stay focused and was easily distracted. He felt that determination would overcome his difficulties. His mother always told him, "If you put your mind to it, you can do it." At the age of thirty-seven, he was diagnosed with AD/HD and placed on medication, which didn't help. During testing, he described the page this way: "It's like you threw the letters up in the air and let them land in some random fashion scattered around the page, next to each other, on top of each other, blurry with glowing auras around each letter." Joseph had constant headaches, like his mother, so he ignored them. During the testing for Irlen Syndrome, he became aware that he got headaches and became tired and anxious when reading or sitting under fluorescent lights. He did not have AD/HD; instead, he had Irlen Syndrome.

—JOSEPH, IRLEN CLIENT FILES

Hyperactivity

Larry is extremely bright and unusually verbal but also very hyperactive. He rarely walks but, instead, jumps almost all the time. Teachers thought that he had AD/HD, so he was given various medications, all without success. Ritalin gave him more energy; so instead of doing three things at the same time, he did five at an even faster speed. Both Larry and his parents collapsed from exhaustion in the evening.

Larry explained that when he tried to read, the letters on the page were "disco dancing." He added that the lighting was poisonous and that everything was always moving. He was constantly moving to keep up with the movement all around him. In time, his parents found out that he did not have AD/HD, but rather that he suffered from Irlen Syndrome, and he was helped by Irlen Filters.

—LARRY, IRLEN CLIENT FILES

Inattentiveness

Ashlee had problems focusing in class. She talked rather than doing her work, she would daydream, and appeared not to be interested in school. In sixth grade she was given medication, but her parents stopped it because it changed her personality. Her parents were inter-

ested in other alternatives. When sitting in class under the lights, things in her environment closed in, glowed brightly, disappeared, and became different shapes. She felt dizzy and kept looking away. She couldn't focus or concentrate, and she felt fidgety and antsy. Now with her Irlen Filters, her mother can see a big difference.

—ASHLEE, IRLEN CLIENT FILES

CONCLUSION

AD/HD and Irlen Syndrome are not the same thing, nor is Irlen Syndrome a type of AD/HD. However, Irlen Syndrome and AD/HD can result in many of the same behaviors. We all are looking for that magic bullet that makes everything alright. The educational system found its magic bullet, expecting that medication would resolve problems of attention, concentration, and lack of focus. The difficulty is that AD/HD is a cluster of behaviors and not a diagnosis. The behaviors can be a result of many different issues. If the behaviors are truly the result of a neurological condition, then medication will be helpful. The problem is that similar behaviors can have a variety of different root causes. Each one, not just Irlen Syndrome, needs to be carefully explored.

Many parents do not feel comfortable with the potential of the side effects of medication. As a result, many parents have chosen to look for alternative options. Alternatives may include counseling, behavior modification, biofeedback, dietary changes, fish oil supplements, vitamins, exercise, and Irlen Spectral Filters. In short, don't jump to conclusions or be pressured into putting your child on medication until you have determined the root of the problem.

In the next chapter, you will discover that some individuals on the autism spectrum have difficulties that involve sensory challenges—one of which can be helped with the Irlen Method.

10

Autism Spectrum Disorder and Irlen Syndrome

> *Although many would support a behavioral view of autism, I have always felt that my son's sensory difficulties were his primary problem and that he's living in a world of misperception.*
>
> —MOTHER OF AN AUTISTIC CHILD

The prevalence of autism has dramatically risen in recent years. In fact, according to the Autism Society of America, the number of children being identified with autism has doubled in the past decade. Recent studies now estimate that 1 in 100 children has autism. It is also expected that along with children, the number of adults with autism will double in the next decade. Everywhere you turn, there are news stories and articles about the increasing number of children being diagnosed. Autism is a critical issue for families, educational systems, and governments, all of which are faced with finding ways to provide for the necessary specialized services this disability requires.

Autism spectrum disorder (ASD) encompasses a variety of developmental disabilities, ranging in severity. This chapter will focus on both those with more severe developmental disorders and those that fall at the milder end of the autism spectrum. The major differences lie in the ability to function in a variety of areas including behavior, social interaction, and communication.

In this chapter, we will explore the link between sensory and visual overload (see page 132) experienced by some individuals on the autism spectrum and the Irlen Method. In addition, this chapter will present

129

descriptions of how these individuals see their world, using the actual words and descriptions from those individuals who can speak for the many who cannot. This chapter also provides an understanding of the reasons behind some of the behaviors associated with this disorder. To be clear, the Irlen Method is *not* a cure for autism, as such cures are still being sought out and researched by scientists and medical experts. The Irlen Method is an effective solution for reducing perceptual sensory overload, thus reducing some of the many challenges these individuals face.

Each individual on the autism spectrum experiences different challenges and symptoms. Therefore, each individual will have different needs for treatment. This chapter will help you identify those who are struggling with the type of sensory overload that can be eliminated with the Irlen Method.

"It is like swimming against the tide and not with it. People look like things thrown at me through the screen of a 3-D movie, and I don't feel safe. Nothing is together, and everything is in pieces," explained one Irlen client.

HOW IT ALL BEGAN

Primarily, the adults who have the language skills and insight into their symptoms have been writing books and speaking at conferences in order to educate professionals, parents, and the public about the nature of their difficulties. I consider these individuals to be the real experts.

In some instances, these same individuals helped me make the connection between sensory overload and the benefits of the Irlen Method for some of those on the autism spectrum. They helped me gain a perspective of exactly what it is like to be living in a distorted world. The first autistic individual to make this connection, back in the mid-1990s, was Donna Williams, an author who has written many books on this subject. What I initially learned from Donna was later reinforced repeatedly by other autistic adults.

Many of the adults with whom I spoke came to see me because they had heard about the Irlen Syndrome and had recognized and resonated with the distortions that happened when reading. However, they came to see me with the hope that Irlen Spectral Filters would be able to calm down their fractured, fragmented world. As the Irlen Method had put a seatbelt on the words to hold them in place, they hoped that the Irlen Filters would be able to stabilize their environment.

I was enlightened by Donna and others who inspired me. I was taken by the hand and led into a world about which I had very little knowledge. I listened and learned. Their distortions were much more extreme than those reported by the college students who I studied back in the 1980s. But, like those students, none of these individuals were aware just how differently they perceived the world compared to the way others saw things.

In the beginning, each adult who wore Irlen Spectral Filters documented the changes that occurred when they put the filters on. I wasn't surprised that they no longer saw a distorted world with their Irlen Filters. They reported that their world was no longer overwhelming, bombarding, and assaulting. Even physical symptoms and anxiety were eliminated. What did come as a surprise, however, was the wide variety of other problems that also improved. Each of these individuals experienced significant improvements not only visually, but in their listening skills, their ability to pull thoughts together, and their ability to communicate. "With my Irlen Filters, the noise in my head stops, and I can more easily hear, listen, think, and talk," explained an Irlen client.

A World of Misperception

The world is a jigsaw puzzle to me, and I can focus on only one piece at a time. None of the pieces are joined together—they are moving; vibrating. I have no faces in my mind, no details, nothing whole. I can see one of your eyes or the other, never both at one time. When I look, I can only see blurred colors that are whirling and sparkling. What I see is only hazy colors; pieces; fragments; nothing whole or detailed. In such a fragmented world, I relate to inanimate objects. Don't try to cure me with therapy while never getting around to my piecemeal perception.

—ASHLEY, TEENAGER WITH ASPERGER'S SYNDROME

Vision trumps all of the other senses. It is estimated that 70 percent of the information people receive enters through the eyes and must be correctly interpreted by the brain, making vision the dominant sense.[1]

Since vision is the sense that provides us with the majority of information we get about our world, any problems in the way we see—or, more accurately, how our brain processes visual information—can cause difficulties in our ability to function in a number of areas. You see what the brain wants you to see. It is interesting to note that children who are blind have similar behaviors in the areas of social interaction, communication, and stereotyped behaviors as those on the autistic spectrum (who can see, but cannot depend on what they see).

As explained to me, their life is like living in a funhouse of distorted mirrors; things are intermittently popping out. This makes bumping and tripping over things that suddenly appear and disappear all too common, which results in feeling anxious and frightened most or all of the time. It is very confusing and disturbing when you cannot trust what you see.

Obviously, visual misperceptions cannot explain all the various impairments associated with autism. However, they may help explain some of the difficulties experienced with social interaction, communication, sensory integration, certain behaviors, and academic pursuits.

Trapped in a Topsy Turvy World of Misperception

Eyes are the windows into the soul, but those on the autistic spectrum have trouble interpreting the view because it is loud, incomprehensible, and bombarding. They describe a distorted world that is different from what their other senses tell them it should be like. It tears apart, portions disappear and reappear, and things are suddenly coming at them, causing a constant state of anxiety. It is a world that is unreliable, inconsistent, fragmented, painful, overwhelming, and frightening. Consequently, they try to filter out the world or shut themselves off from the world. The

---

Visual Overload

A survey conducted in 1994 by the Geneva Centre for Autism in Toronto, Canada—and published in a pamphlet titled *The Sensory Experiences of Individuals with Autism Based on First Hand Accounts*—found that even though distortions and visual overload are not considered a significant issue by the professionals, 81 percent of those on the autistic spectrum studied reported distorted perception.[2] The most common problems were:

- Difficulties with depth perception
- Distorted perception of size, shape, and motion
- Distraction
- Seeing only small details and not the whole
- Visual over-stimulation

following sections are some of the more common areas in which they have problems.

Communicating

Seeing and hearing are connected. In a world where things are constantly distorting and changing, the ability to concentrate and put words together in sentences becomes difficult. Thus, the ability to communicate with others and carry on a conversation becomes impossible. Some clients report that thoughts just stop and that headaches and dizziness take over.

Depth Perception

"My eyes lie to me," is how one client expressed this difficulty. They cannot trust or depend on what they see to be correct, and it rarely is. This results in difficulty judging heights, distance, speed, and spatial awareness. Although poor depth perception is a problem for many of the populations that the Irlen Method helps, for those with autism, these difficulties are so much more disturbing. Some of our clients report that they see their world, and everything in their environment, as flat but also with pieces missing, flying apart, and melding together like Jell-O. Some clients report that even walking is frightening because the bumps, cracks, or changes in levels disappear and reappear. Even worse is always feeling anxious, fearful of tripping and falling because it feels like stepping into space.

Hearing

It is hard to hear when you are living in a disjointed world. Sounds become muffled and unclear, and individuals can have trouble understanding what people are saying. Facial expression and body language aid hearing; but many of our clients do not see faces, only holes where mouths and eyes should be, and arms that split apart. Not only are they missing visual clues, but they are working at blocking out what they see and cannot listen at the same time. One client reported, "The world is essentially fragmented with lots of blind spots. My brain tries to fill in the gaps. I cannot listen properly as I am mainly trying to make sense of what I am seeing."

Light Sensitivity

Our clients report that they are not just bothered but rather are tortured by lighting. It doesn't have to be sunlight, bright lights, or fluorescent lights; any lighting increases the visual fragmentation and creates extreme physical pain. "In light, my eyes feel like they are full of razor blades. I cannot see things, only colors of light, the flicker, and flashes," a client reported.

Reading and Academics

Distractibility while reading and doing academic tasks can also be a problem for those on the autism spectrum. But, like other aspects of autism, the severity of the issue varies depending on the individual. Some people with autism have good reading skills. Others may read fast but with very little comprehension. Many people lose their place while reading or copying, or they simply cannot copy fast enough from the board at school.

Viewing People

When I look at you, you distort, so part of your face disappears and the other part stretches out, so you look evil and distorted and I don't want to look at you.

—SEAN, IRLEN CLIENT FILES

Figure 10.1. Distorted Faces Without Irlen Filters. This picture was submitted by an autistic Irlen client. It represents the way she perceives faces when she is not wearing her Irlen Filters.

For autistic people, faces are the most difficult part of a person to perceive and are extremely frightening. Some descriptions our clients have shared with us include faces that look like blobs with black holes where the eyes and mouth should be (see Figures 10.1 and 10.2); ghosting faces that are blank or empty with no features; faces with multiple images; faces that appear as jigsaw puzzles with pieces missing; and faces with piercing eyes that look frightening. Not only are the faces hard to see, but parts of a person's body may appear to be missing so that the individual looks disjointed. Thus, it is impossible for some individuals on the autism spectrum to recognize people and see facial expressions and body language. Often, it becomes a choice of looking but not seeing, or looking away and simply listening.

Viewing the World

Nothing in my world is whole and recognizable, and I cannot tell what I am seeing. The sensory bombardment feels like being hit by a tidal wave.

—BILL, IRLEN CLIENT FILES

Figure 10.2. Non-Distorted Faces With Irlen Filters. This picture was submitted by the same client who drew Figure 10.1. It represents how she views people's faces when she is wearing her Irlen Filters.

Some of our clients describe the world as jumbled; fragmented with missing pieces, multiple images, items that disappear and suddenly reappear, and objects that appear to come toward them, which results in a feeling of being attacked. The environment is confusing, scary, dizzy, and nauseating. The world becomes a combination of meaningless colors, forms, and movement. It is impossible to get meaning from their perception; impossible to understand what they see.

Seeing Movement

Moving things become an unintelligible blur with tons of after-images and bright flashes.

—MEG, IRLEN CLIENT FILES

Movement adds an additional layer of sensory overload, making an already chaotic world incomprehensible. This causes problems even doing the simplest of tasks, such as getting on or off escalators, crossing a street, or catching a bus.

Social Situations

An autistic person's inability to understand social nuances and interact appropriately in social situations (and the tendency to misinterpret social situations) can be related to a difficulty seeing facial expressions and body language. As a result, they often misunderstand—or completely overlook—the meaning, the implied message, or the emotion behind the message. This makes it difficult to know how to interact properly with people. Instead, some of our clients mimic words and movements. Just as when people are in a foreign culture and do not know how to act, they copy the actions or mannerisms of those around them.

THE REASONS BEHIND THE BEHAVIORS

Those on the autistic spectrum use many different behaviors to calm down and reduce the stress, panic, and anxiety they feel (see inset on opposite page). Some are ritualistic and can include rhythmic and repetitive behaviors, such as self-stimming, finger flicking, rocking, head banging, spinning, and arm flapping. These are typically unconscious behaviors that can soothe or regulate. The mesmerizing effect of sparkles, spinning, and moving objects can also be very calming.

Other behaviors—such as looking only in short glances, looking down or away, squinting, looking sideways at a person or object, and

---

Physical Symptoms

Major visual disorientation and fragmented vision are accompanied by feelings of total disorientation and panic. Similarly, living with constant sensory bombardment can result in anxiety, feelings of being threatened, outbursts of anger, aggressive behavior, and even screaming, wailing, running away, and swearing when the familiar becomes unrecognizable. Just as those misdiagnosed with anxiety and panic disorders retreat from sensory overload by going to safe environments, those with autism may also retreat—but into themselves, blocking out the world around them.

---

avoiding eye contact—reduce or eliminate the pain and bombardment of the environment.

Things suddenly appear and jump towards me like they are going to attack me. I feel scared, and I panic. I just want to retreat from the chaos because it's just overwhelming. I have to look away or only in short glances.

—RYAN, IRLEN CLIENT FILES

There are other behaviors used to help make sense of a distorted environment, such as feeling, touching, and tasting. When vision isn't reliable, it is not uncommon to use other senses to understand, orient oneself, or get a feeling for what is going on. These other senses can help you "see."

Rather than look at things, I will rub them, touch them, or put them to my face to try to understand what they are.

—JILLIAN, IRLEN CLIENT FILES

Finally, there are behaviors that indicate when an individual is experiencing discomfort, such as squinting, rubbing or pushing on her eyes, and hitting her eyes. All of these behaviors can indicate the type of sensory overload that can be eliminated with Irlen Spectral Filters.

The Problem With Treatment

Professionals have difficulty understanding the importance of reducing visual overload. Yet, when those with autism talk about their problems, they mention sensory sensitivities and sensory overload as major issues and that the behaviors they exhibit are symptoms, masking a bigger problem. One individual said, "Instead of trying to change or control my behaviors so that I look more normal to you, try to find out what is causing these behaviors and fix that."

Fortunately, individuals on the autism spectrum, especially the adults, are now speaking at conferences and educating professionals and parents about their problems and struggles. This has opened the door to a greater understanding of what living with autism spectrum disorders is like. These individuals present the world through their eyes and serve as a guiding light, sharing their insights and information.

Nonetheless, certain therapies can be counterproductive. For example, training someone with autism to look at you while you are talking may not be helpful because it does not take into account *why* the individual is not looking at you. It does not take into account that looking produces confusion, pain, and discomfort. Such therapy may make the individual appear normal to others, but it may not be helpful. These therapies are merely training behaviors that do not actually eliminate the problem. As one individual on the autism spectrum explained, "I've learned to look at you without really looking. But everything is so chaotic and disturbing that I can only see blurs of colors."

Some individuals with autism have told me that although they know it is inappropriate to walk around without shoes, they prefer to take off their shoes. Being barefooted allows them to get reliable and consistent information about their environment to compensate for the unreliable information they get from a distorted visual world. "I don't see cracks or curbs or stairs or pebbles. The world is frightening," one client explained. Therapies that "teach" them to conform may make those with autism appear to be more "normal." However, they do nothing to alleviate the real problem—their fragmented, distorted world. In fact, these therapies can make life even more stressful by taking away coping strategies.

Likewise, should we eliminate the self-stimming behaviors that are used as a means of calming and relieving tension because they are not "normal"? Wouldn't it better serve this population to minimize the sensory overload that is causing a need for these behaviors?

From a societal viewpoint, the common thinking is if you look like everyone else, you will function better. Too often we feel that how someone looks or acts best reflects who they are and how they feel; in reality, it only makes those of us watching, or interacting with the person, more comfortable. The question still remains: Wouldn't it be better to eliminate the cause of the behaviors rather than changing the behaviors?

Addressing Sensory Overload with the Irlen Method

I know of several children and adults (with Asperger's Syndrome) who have reported a considerable reduction in visual sensitivity and sensory overload when wearing Irlen [Filters].

—TONY ATTWOOD, PhD, EXPERT IN THE FIELD OF ASPERGER'S SYNDROME AND AUTHOR OF *A COMPLETE GUIDE TO ASPERGER'S SYNDROME*

Although there are therapies to address tactile and auditory sensitivities, only the Irlen Method addresses the behaviors and difficulties related to perceptual sensitivities and sensory overload that many with autism face. The Irlen Method achieves changes without weekly or daily therapy sessions. Unlike many of the other therapies, the Irlen Method does not require skill development or the unlearning of behaviors, nor does the individual with autism need to be trained to learn different behaviors. The emphasis is not placed on making the individual "look normal," but, instead, on eliminating the perceptual reasons for the behaviors. By eliminating the need to block out or reduce sensory overload, more appropriate—or acceptable— behaviors automatically replace the behaviors that result from sensory overload. This can be achieved by wearing Irlen Spectral Filters.

Irlen Spectral Filters are only one part of a successful treatment plan—one piece of the puzzle, if you will. Unfortunately, Irlen Spectral Filters will not help everyone on the autism spectrum. Only those who suffer from a specific type of sensory sensitivity benefit from this method and are tested for Irlen Filters. Therefore, we have developed prescreening methods to identify those who can be helped.

Parents often ask, "Can you actually test individuals if they have little or no language or if they have behaviors that interfere with their ability to cooperate?" The answer is yes. Testing is not dependent solely upon the individual's ability to communicate. Therefore, children who are unable to talk, have difficulty understanding what you ask, or have problems expressing how they feel can still be tested. Testing does not require the child to follow directions or answer questions. Certified Irlen Diagnosticians are specially trained to be able to work with people who are a part of the autistic population.

As a means of pre-determining if the Irlen Method can be beneficial, we have developed an autism questionnaire, which asks about the behaviors and problems that are associated with the type of sensory sensitivities that can be improved with Irlen Filters. This autism questionnaire can be found on www.irlen.com.

In addition, for young children or those with limited or no language, there are a series of activities using different colored light bulbs that can be done. These activities are also found on the Irlen website and can be completed at home. For those who *can* be helped with Irlen Filters, there will be noticeable, positive changes with certain colored bulbs and negative changes with other colors. We have found that there is a high correlation between the positive changes in behavior that occur when changing the color of the light bulb and the changes that occur with Irlen Filters (although the color of the light bulb that has a positive effect will not be the same as the color of Irlen Spectral Filters).

REAL LIFE STORIES: IN THE EYES OF THE BEHOLDER

In this section, you will be able to read the words of those who struggle with sensory overload. Luckily, Irlen Filters can help (see opposite page).

It is almost impossible to imagine what it is like to live in a chaotic world that is unpredictable, always giving you the wrong information, and leaving you in a constant state of anxiety, panic, and fear. In this section, you will be able to read the words of people who live like this every day (indicated in italics).

- Communicating. *My vision is always going on and off; my hearing also goes on and off and I can't think, pull my thoughts together, or carry on a conversation. It's impossible to concentrate.*

- Depth perception. *It is frightening trying to walk down steps that look like they are not there. It's also frightening and frustrating constantly bumping into tables, walls, and doors; tripping, falling over things, and misjudging heights because I cannot see things. Stairs are seen as sheer, and it feels as if I am walking off a mountain.*

- Hearing. *When you speak, it all sounds like, "blah, blah, blah." I have a terrible headache and can't concentrate, which prevents me from seeing, hearing, and even thinking clearly.*

- Light sensitivity. *Reflections bounce off everything, making the room into a constant light show. Sparkles and colors dance around so that all I can see are the sparkles and colors of light.*

- Reading and academics. *My eyes are not able to read each word in a line without flying off and scanning other words on the page.*

- Social situations. *I try to memorize pieces and form a whole image. This is impossible to do; and so, as a result, I usually misread social cues. This leads*

Common Reports of Changes
with Irlen Spectral Filters

When dealing with people on the autism spectrum, there are a number of areas that tend to improve with the use of Irlen Spectral Filters. Of course, since problems vary depending on the individual, the amount and areas of improvement will also vary.

The following are the most common areas of change that we have seen in children and adults:

- Academic skills. Skills such as copying, doing math problems, and reading are more accurate when Irlen Spectral Filters come into play.

- Behavioral changes. Many times, the individual is calmer and less anxious with Irlen Filters. Some individuals feel better because they no longer experience chronic physical symptoms, such as fear, panic, anxiety, headaches, or dizziness.

- Depth perception. Many people experience changes in certain skills that involve depth perception. For example, going up and down stairs is easier and hand-eye coordination improves. Additionally, many people who used to have trouble walking along the street will no longer walk off curbs or bump into things when they are wearing their Irlen Filters. Some individuals go from seeing a flat world to suddenly being able to see a world that is three-dimensional.

- Hearing. The Irlen Filters eliminate the visual overload that interfere with both seeing and hearing. Since the other senses are no longer working overtime, the ability to hear sounds and voices improves.

- Light sensitivity. Irlen Filter wearers are much better able to tolerate fluorescent light, sunlight, and bright lights. Lighting no longer causes physical symptoms, and the world is calmer and together without distortions.

- Social interaction. The increased ability to see faces correctly and interpret emotions makes it easier to socialize.

- Thinking. Concentration and the ability to focus become easier when there is less sensory overload.

to anxiety. My inability to see faces and body language leads to inappropriate responses. Sometimes I take total control of the conversation so I don't have to respond.

I could feel the water +
hear the bubbles. I stepped
into a space like air. I could
feel the bath tub

Figure 10.3: Viewing the World Without Irlen Filters. This picture was submitted by an autistic Irlen client. It represents how she perceives taking a bath when she is not wearing her Irlen Filters.

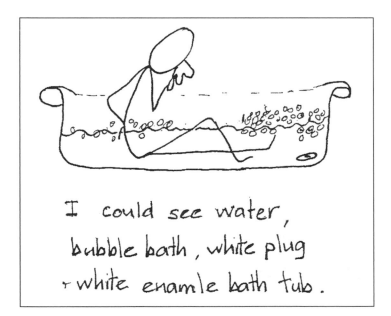

I could see water,
bubble bath, white plug
+ white enamle bath tub.

Figure 10.4: Viewing the World With Irlen Filters. This picture was submitted by the same client who drew Figure 10.3. It represents how she feels taking a bath when she is wearing her Irlen Filters.

- Viewing people. *"I can only recognize a person by their voice and have to wait until they speak,"* one young man explained. Others have reported that they can tell people apart by the way they walk. *"My father slides, my mother walks slowly, and my brother goes klunk, klunk, klunk,"* explains a teenager.

- Viewing the world. *Taking a bath is alarming because I not only feel bombarded by everything, but I only see parts of me in bits and pieces and can't see the water.* (See Figures 10.3 and 10.4.) *My only escape from the intolerable and impossible world of seeing is to escape by tuning out or shutting down.*

CONCLUSION

While research continues to focus on cures, families are left to try a variety of treatments including behavioral therapy, occupational therapy, physical therapy, sensory integration therapy, social skills classes, sound therapies, and speech and language therapies. Others are finding help with more natural alternatives including amino acids, enzymes, probiotics, antifungal and celation, gluthathine IV, B_{12} shots, Finegold's diet, a gluten and casein-free diet, supplements, hyperbaric oxygen therapy, and medication to regulate the immune system and reduce anxiety. Individuals with autism often benefit from one or a combination of these therapies, but none address the sensory issues that are discussed in this chapter and have been helped with the Irlen Method.

While the hope of parents worldwide is that there will soon be a cure, those living with autism need immediate solutions to the sensory overload they experience. The Irlen Method is not a cure for those on the autistic spectrum—but until a cure is found, it does offer relief for perceptual sensory problems and sensory overload.

In the next chapter, you will learn about certain medical and visual conditions that also create sensory overload, causing Irlen-like symptoms. These symptoms, like so many others we've talked about, can also be helped by the Irlen Method.

11

Medical Conditions, Visual Conditions, and Irlen Syndrome

> *At the age of forty-four, I had a stroke. Since the stroke, my eyes have started bouncing and crossing. I see double and become nauseous. I started listening to books on tape because I could no longer read comfortably.*
>
> *My world had changed, and I missed reading. After four months of using Irlen Filters, my eyes no longer hurt or bounce around, and I am, once again, able to read.*
>
> —CHARLES, STROKE VICTIM AND IRLEN CLIENT

In previous chapters, we have discussed symptoms and problems related to Irlen Syndrome. We explained that this specific type of processing deficit is genetic and is therefore often passed on from one generation to the next.

In this chapter, we will talk about the same symptoms that have been discussed in other chapters. However, rather than the cause being inherited, these problems have occurred as a result of certain medical or visual conditions. The conditions discussed in this chapter have symptoms mirroring those of Irlen Syndrome, very similar to the symptoms discussed in the previous chapters. (For more on the difference between acquired and inherited, see page 146.)

This chapter does not suggest that the Irlen Method is a cure for medical or visual disorders, nor does it suggest that the Irlen Method will eliminate the need for medication or therapies required to address these conditions. Likewise, the Irlen Method will not reverse the course of a disease. It is essential that any medical or visual conditions be fully investigated by a doctor to ensure that all possible medical treatments are undertaken. However, the use of the Irlen Method should not be dismissed in the presence of pathology.

What this chapter does do is point out some less obvious—and often overlooked—symptoms of certain medical and visual conditions that can be lessened or eliminated by the Irlen Method, providing the individual with an increased ability to perform and to enjoy both greater comfort and a better quality of life.

MEDICAL CONDITIONS

Medical conditions can have a cluster of symptoms, some of which are considered relevant and treatable, while others may be dismissed as unimportant or not treatable. It is these primarily overlooked symptoms that we will be focusing on in this chapter.

Over the years, we have received phone calls and emails from thousands of people who identify with the symptoms of Irlen Syndrome, wondering if they, too, could be helped. Some felt that they had always had mild symptoms of Irlen Syndrome that were made worse by their medical or visual problems. Others knew that they never had these problems until an illness or accident changed their life. Regardless, they were all seeking a solution.

The Major Difference Between Acquired and Inherited

We have found one dramatic difference between the individuals with Irlen Syndrome, which is hereditary, and those who have acquired Irlen-like symptoms: the latter have a very clear means of comparison. When we spoke with people who had acquired Irlen-like symptoms later in life, we were talking with clients who knew what reading was like before their illness or injury, so they had a point of reference from which to compare and tell us very clearly that things were not right any longer. They knew that words were not supposed to move or disappear. They knew that they used to be able to read for hours and no longer could. They knew that lighting had not bothered them before. These individuals could recall the way life used to be. Because of this, it was easier to help these people, since they knew how things were supposed to be. They knew what it would be like to feel better.

Initially, we did not know whether the Irlen Method would work as well when the symptoms were not a result of Irlen Syndrome, but rather simply Irlen-like symptoms.

Medical Problems and Environmental Triggers

When a person suffers from an injury or illness, *all* the possible symptoms and complications that can result from said illness should be recognized. Additionally, any medical diagnosis must include a list of all, not just some, of the symptoms the individual is experiencing since some of the symptoms may be triggered by lighting or other environmental sources and can, therefore, be controlled.

Environmental triggers can exacerbate some medical conditions. Irlen-like symptoms that accompany certain medical illnesses can include light sensitivity, strain, discomfort, fatigue, anxiety, and reading and depth perception problems, among others. Although medication may be helpful, some symptoms may not improve with therapy and/or psychotropic medication.

The problem for many individuals is that in the course of dealing with their medical condition, they are told by a professional that certain symptoms are part of the condition and will persist until their medical condition subsides. This is not necessarily the case. If you now find that certain environmental triggers create discomfort, perceptual distortions, anxiety, and other symptoms, these problems can be controlled and often eliminated. Use your knowledge to assess your symptoms and see if you can rule out some causes of your symptoms. Try altering your environment to see if you feel any better by changing the lighting around you. Be aware if you do feel calmer or better in rooms that are dimly lit rather than with bright fluorescent lighting. Determine if you feel like you need more light. Pay attention to whether reading or other visual tasks are easier, or if it is easier to concentrate and follow conversations. While you may not be able to eliminate the actual illness or problem, you will feel better by focusing on getting rid of some of the symptoms that aggravate it.

Medical Conditions and Irlen-Like Symptoms

As we get closer to the deadline for eliminating incandescent lighting (see page 93), the number of websites, blogs, and petitions focusing on the problems of fluorescent lighting increases. Most of the postings are from people with a variety of medical and visual conditions who experience severe headaches, stomachaches, nausea, dizziness, fatigue, eye strain, anxiety, irritability, and other physical symptoms when under fluorescent lighting. Each individual complains about the serious nature of their symptoms and is desperately seeking a solution. These individuals express real frustration with the medical profession because many times light sensitivity is dismissed as an insignificant symptom. These people feel that doctors and others in the medical field are not recognizing or giving credence to the severity of their symptoms. They feel like they are left alone to try to find a solution, and many turn to the web for answers.

Seeking a solution to their symptoms is exactly how many people finally discover the Irlen Method. After spending hours and days searching the web, those who are lucky stumble across a link to www.irlen.com. Many of these people later tell me they immediately identified with one or more of the various symptoms associated with Irlen Syndrome, which is what led them to make an appointment.

I have been surprised at the range of medical conditions that can trigger Irlen-like symptoms, including light-induced epilepsy, stroke, chronic fatigue syndrome, autoimmune diseases, multiple sclerosis, cerebral palsy, fibromyalgia, lupus, viral illnesses, Tourette's Syndrome, lyme disease, viral meningitis, spina bifida, toxic overload, and mercury poisoning. Remember, when we say that we have "treated" people with these ailments, we are referring to eliminating the symptoms to make life much more manageable, *not* curing the actual illness.

Unexplained medical symptoms account for roughly $20 billion in United States healthcare costs each year. Research may find ways to cure some of these mysterious ailments, but this still leaves those suffering from unidentified issues without answers. However, eliminating the symptoms that mirror those of Irlen Syndrome can result in increased energy, less fatigue, improved overall health, and fewer doctor visits.

The positive changes are usually quick and long-lasting, provided that the Irlen Filters are worn regularly. In fact, once the debilitating symptoms are removed, many people feel as if a great weight has been lifted from their shoulders, allowing them to focus on treating or gaining control over the actual illness. For example, it is easier to keep up a recommended regular exercise program when not having to deal with chronic headaches along with your other medical symptoms.

The following sections detail some of the medical conditions that have brought clients to us for help. In each case, the Irlen Method provided relief only for the physical and perceptual symptoms, making it easier for the individual to focus on the main issue.

Cerebral Palsy (CP)

CP is the term for a group of disorders that affect an individual's ability to coordinate body movements. It may cause muscles to be weak and floppy or rigid and stiff. We hear from parents who are not sure if their child's academic issues are caused by CP, a learning problem, or Irlen Syndrome. They are thankful that we could easily determine if the cause is Irlen Syndrome or not. For Madison, a child who we tested, the Irlen Method settled down the moving numbers and letters that made her nauseous and caused her learning difficulty. Stories such as Madison's are encouraging because they mean that more people are taking matters into their own hands, searching the internet to find help for their symptoms, discovering the Irlen Method, and finding that there is a solution for some of their symptoms.

Another parent, Carolyn, wrote to us about her son who has CP:

We noticed that he turns off the living room and kitchen lights. He says, "The light bothers me." I have asked and asked questions about this, getting no help from the physician, ophthalmologist, or optometrist. Irlen Filters were the solution, and I cried when my son said, "Mommy, you mean the letters weren't supposed to be dancing?"

—CAROLYN, IRLEN CLIENT FILES

Chronic Fatigue Syndrome (CFS)

CFS is an autoimmune disorder characterized by prolonged, debilitating fatigue and multiple nonspecific symptoms such as headaches, muscle and joint pain, and memory and concentration problems. I have worked with adults with CFS who knew they had always experienced severe light sensitivity, physical symptoms, and reading and attention struggles. Many also had learning difficulties. They reported that as long as they could remember, they had been pushing themselves to perform through the fatigue and through serious physical symptoms. They kept pushing forward until their systems could not take it any more. For years, they kept putting themselves under chronic stress, expecting to function while compromising their immune systems. Then, suddenly, the system just crashes.

CFS, however, is unique. We have found that, in some cases, severe and untreated Irlen Syndrome may lead to CFS; while in other instances, CFS can lead to Irlen-like symptoms.

Additionally, there are those who have Irlen Syndrome and find that their symptoms become worse after developing CFS. This is what happened to Eve, an Irlen client.

I have always been extremely light sensitive, and this is something that has become even more intense since I have had CFS. Now, I cannot leave the house, summer or winter, without my wrap-around sunglasses firmly over my eyes. Over the last three years, I've had increasing difficulty with reading print from a page for any length of time. This has been a mind-boggling and utterly weird development because I've always been a voracious and very successful reader. I can only conclude that CFS has either exacerbated a minimal level of Irlen Syndrome, which I feel I've always had, or that it has pre-cipitated a full-blown version of Irlen Syndrome in its own right. Whatever the answer, I'm profoundly grateful to have discovered something that so simply alleviates this condition. Without the research connecting Irlen Syndrome to CFS, this disabling aspect of CFS would not have been brought to light.

—EVE, IRLEN CLIENT FILES

Environmental Toxicity

Environmental toxicity affects people who are exposed to toxic materials. We have seen a number of clients who suffer from different environmental toxicities. Most have started or completed a detox program; but many times academic problems, difficulty focusing, light sensitivity, and fatigue continue afterwards. These individuals experience a number of physical symptoms when under fluorescent lighting, including anxiety, irritability, and fatigue. In addition, reading, writing, and copying become challenging; and they experience perceptual distortions that are quite significant. Some become exhausted, some shut down, some can no longer think or function, some experience tics, and some suffer from headaches or dizziness when under fluorescent lights.

Fibromyalgia

Nearly 6 million Americans suffer from fibromyalgia, a chronic illness characterized by widespread muscle pain, fatigue, and multiple tender points throughout the body. This little-understood, often-frustrating illness can have symptoms that include fatigue, sleep disturbances, depression, headaches, irritable bowel syndrome, and heightened sensitivity.

A client who had been wearing Irlen Filters for a number of years came in to see me and said that she was wondering if anyone had ever checked to see how many Irlen clients also had fibromyalgia. She was sure that there was a connection because both she and her daughter had fibromyalgia, and they found it to be interesting that so many of their symptoms were kept under control as long as they are wearing their Irlen Filters.

She was right. We discovered that there was a correlation between Irlen Syndrome and some of the problems associated with fibromyalgia, such as light sensitivity, eye pain, distorted vision, fluctuating visual clarity, anxiety, and fatigue. Thus, it seemed reasonable that the Irlen Method would be helpful for some people with fibromyalgia since protecting the brain from additional stress would also protect the immune system. As we have expanded beyond helping those with reading difficulties to helping other populations, we have found that it is our clients who have helped us to identify the different illnesses or medical problems that have Irlen-like symptoms and respond to wearing Irlen Filters.

Light-Sensitive Epilepsy

Light-sensitive epilepsy is also known as photosensitive epilepsy. Seizures are triggered by visual stimuli such as patterns, flashing or flickering lights, and stripes. Both artificial and natural light may trigger seizures. TV, video games, fluorescent lighting, flashing from light to dark, and passing by picket fences are common triggers. Although people with light-sensitive epilepsy have not inherited Irlen Syndrome, they have the same triggers and often find that Irlen Filters reduce these sensitivities.

Irlen client Kelli wrote us a letter about how the Irlen Filters helped her overcome her symptoms associated with light-sensitive epilepsy:

I have recently heard of Irlen Filters and their effectiveness in areas where I need help. I have problems reading, studying, remembering details, and with bright lights—especially since I have epilepsy. My medication has never totally controlled my seizures. I have constant headaches and balance problems and have been told that there is nothing that can be done to improve my situation. I don't want to take drugs that don't work for the rest of my life, especially since other forces may be at work here. It was wonderful to learn that Irlen Filters could help with my symptoms.

—KELLI, IRLEN CLIENT FILES

Tourette's Syndrome (TS)

Ongoing research indicates that TS is a neurological disorder related to an abnormal metabolism of the neurotransmitters dopamine and serotonin. Most people with TS experience motor and vocal tics that change in number, frequency, type, and location. Typically, the tics increase as a result of tension or stress.

The question brought to our attention, by the first client we saw with TS, was whether some of her behavioral, educational, and attention problems associated with TS were triggered by environmental factors and, if so, could they be helped by the Irlen Method. She had read that the Irlen Method could alter the biochemistry of the brain by calming it down so that the neurotransmitters (such as dopamine and serotonin) would reach more "normal" levels. She was hoping that by decreasing stress from the environment, she would have less tic activity. For this patient, glare, fluorescent lighting, sunlight, driving, and computer screens were stressful and increased the frequency and severity of her tics.

After six months of wearing Irlen Filters all the time, she reported to us that they had not eliminated the need for her medicine, and she was still experiencing tics. However, wearing Irlen Filters reduced the amount of visual stimulation, which meant that her tics were neither as violent nor as intense as they had been. Her tic activity, when on the computer, reading, and doing other visual activities, was significantly reduced. In addition, reading was easier for her since the words no longer were moving.

VISUAL DISORDERS

Individuals with a variety of visual conditions, visual impairments, and eye diseases have also sought out the Irlen Method because symptoms, including sensitivity to lights and glare, visual distortions, visual discomfort and reading problems, have led them to discovering Irlen Syndrome. We have successfully helped these symptoms in people with retinitis pigmentosa (RP), cataracts, degenerative eye diseases, and macular degeneration. Some individuals with visual impairments including low vision, nystagmus, strabismus, alternative suppression, and binocular dysfunction have also been helped.

Visual Disorders and Irlen-Like Symptoms

Before discussing how the Irlen Method has proven beneficial to individuals with visual disorders, it is important to remember that Irlen Syndrome is not itself a visual disorder, but rather a perceptual processing disorder. The Irlen Method does not replace the care and attention of a vision specialist, nor will it be able to reverse the effects of the pathology or disease.

Light Sensitivity, Glare, and Contrast Sensitivity

Lighting and glare can be major factors that affect vision. Reflected glare from glossy surfaces, such as paper, desktops, walls and/or cabinets, can be very bothersome for many people who have visual conditions or low vision. One of the common recommendations for reducing the symptoms is to simply wear sunglasses—the darker the better. The problem with sunglasses, however, is that they not only reduce brightness, but also reduce the overall amount of light, making it darker and harder to see for the person wearing them. Individuals who are already struggling to see may strain even more with sunglasses. The ideal result is to provide these individuals with greater comfort without reducing vision. Irlen Spectral Filters do not darken your world, but they do provide some degree of increased comfort.

Legally Blind

There are nearly 2 million individuals in the United States who are classified as legally blind. Despite popular misconception, being blind does not only mean that you cannot see anything.

Here at Irlen, we have helped legally blind individuals in a number of different ways, including reducing or eliminating the constant light show of colors and flashing lights that some individuals see, which have been known to trigger chronic headaches.

One woman, Lilly, describes her situation in this touching letter:

I may be blind, but I see shadow and motion. The downside is the accompanying light show that I endure. Fourth of July fireworks are nothing when compared to the display of flashing lights I see every day. Perhaps a better way to describe the effect would be to compare it to sunlight dancing on moving water. As a result, I often experience severe headaches and fatigue. Fluorescent lights are especially annoying.

In the past, I had been told that my light show was an unavoidable fact of life. Doctors had no solution, and I have suffered with this discomfort for so long. Recently, I was introduced to Irlen Filters, and I found a color combination that decreased the light show by around 80 percent. Since I started using my filters, my headaches have also decreased dramatically. My shadow vision has increased as well.

I have found the filters to be a qualified success. They cannot help me see, but they do help me have a better and less painful life.

—LILLY, IRLEN CLIENT FILES

Low Vision

Nearly 4 million people in the United States have low vision and other visual impairments. These individuals have some functional vision that they can use, but often use aids such as telescopic eyewear, magnifiers, adaptive equipment, and closed circuit television systems. Sometimes, amber or yellow glasses are prescribed to assist and support individuals with low vision, most of which address color, contrast, and illumination. However, such interventions typically assume that "one size fits all," giving everyone the same color. But contrary to popular belief, the needs of children and adults with low vision vary. These needs have to be determined on an individual basis, just as vision needs to be addressed with individual prescriptions for each person wearing glasses or contact lenses.

The significant difference between colored glasses typically provided to those with low vision and Irlen Spectral Filters is that the Irlen Filters are fine-tuned so that the color is specifically created to best benefit the person wearing them. Colored glasses may provide some relief, but Irlen Filters—specifically selected for each individual—provide much greater relief. Additionally, Irlen Filters do not reduce clarity or contrast, which can sometimes happen with colored glasses.

The Irlen Method has been introduced to the low vision population to increase the efficiency with which they can use their functional vision. Over time, we have found that Irlen Spectral Filters help in a variety of areas, including:

- Cutting glare (including scattered glare) and reflections

- Enhancing contrast

- Enhancing patterns and outlines

- Providing greater clarity

- Providing increased comfort

As a result, the Irlen Filters help many of those who have low vision and other visual impairments, providing additional ease and comfort while using their residual vision.

Since 2001, Fritz Steiner, Director for the Institute for the Visually Impaired in Switzerland, has documented the benefits Irlen Filters can have on the visually impaired including those with low vision. In summarizing his results, he writes:

> I have noticed that 60 percent of the visually impaired individuals I have tested have benefited from the use of Irlen Filters. Nearly all of those individuals report greater eye comfort, less muscle tension, greater ability to do visual work for long periods of time, and a decreased disturbance from reduced contrast. The Irlen [Filters] have these people maximize their residual vision.

Macular Degeneration

Associated primarily with seniors, macular degeneration (MD) results in deteriorated or blurred vision and can ultimately cause blindness.

When I first heard about Irlen Filters, I got very excited because I had the feeling that the filters could also help me take away a layer of the fog. The Irlen Filters did give me more comfort. I am able to see much more in the bright sunlight. At night, while riding in a car, the lights are less offensive, no longer being halo-like blobs. Additionally, when I am using my computer for an extended amount of time, my Irlen Filters help to sharpen the image and lessen eye strain. The most amazing aspect of wearing my new filters is that I have fewer headaches than ever before.

—HELEN, IRLEN CLIENT FILES

When someone with a visual condition calls for an appointment, I am always very careful to explain what the Irlen Method can and cannot do. For those with macular degeneration and other visual conditions, I always want the client to be aware that we cannot change the course of the disease or reverse the lost vision. What we can do, however, is bring a certain amount of relief and comfort, especially in bright lighting, from glare, and for some people who have trouble with movement and sparkles. For those with visual conditions, the amount of relief will vary but will never be 100 percent.

Other Visual Disorders

We have treated clients with a variety of visual conditions that resulted in light sensitivity, reduced vision, and sometimes physical symptoms. As mentioned earlier in this chapter, we cannot reverse the effects of a degenerative disease. However, many times we have been able to help patients by reducing some of their symptoms, making it easier for them to deal with daily life.

One woman who came to us recalls her story.

My retinas were already damaged by retinopathy. I did not expect miracles [when I went to the Irlen Clinic] and was only hoping for some gains and comfort. I was evaluated, determined that the method would be helpful, and received my Irlen Filters.

The greatest rewards I experienced with my filters were the small things, such as seeing my first single snowflakes, knowing what someone really looks like, seeing the color of a friend's eyes, seeing facial expressions, and finding a bird as it sits in a tree.

—CRYSTAL, IRLEN CLIENT FILES

People who suffer with symptoms of light sensitivity as a result of eye surgery have also contacted us for assistance. One woman wrote about her husband's response to Lasik eye surgery. While Lasik does improve vision, it can sometimes cause light sensitivity.

Following the surgery, my husband became very "light sensitive." He said that his ability to read diminished, and he was no longer comfortable in bright lights. After visiting an Irlen Clinic and undergoing an evaluation, he received rose-colored filters. His Irlen Filters have helped him accentuate individual letters on the written page, while also making it more comfortable for him to read and to be outside.

—MURIEL, IRLEN CLIENT FILES

CONCLUSION

Clearly, we have seen that some symptoms associated with various medical and visual conditions mirror those of Irlen Syndrome. As a result, Irlen Spectral Filters have played a role in improving the quality of life for numerous individuals suffering from such symptoms.

Of course, the first course of action for anyone with medical or visual problems is to get medical attention. Your first goal should always be to treat or cure the condition. What happens, however, is that very often, ongoing symptoms persist; and other than over-the-counter products designed for short-term help, individuals do not know where to turn for comfort and relief from Irlen-like symptoms. In this case, Irlen Filters may be a solution. The Irlen Spectral Filters have been successful, as illustrated by the stories in this chapter, for people, minimizing—and often eliminating—certain lingering symptoms resulting from such conditions.

In some cases, for medical conditions for which there are no cure, Irlen Filters have resulted in making life that much easier and more comfortable for those afflicted. In fact, much of the research and learning has come from the individuals who seek out Irlen for the symptoms associated with a wide range of medical conditions.

In the following chapter, we will discuss the relationship that often exists between head injuries, psychological problems, and Irlen Syndrome, and we will explore how the Irlen Method can help.

12

Head Injuries, Psychological Problems, and Irlen Syndrome

> *Irlen Syndrome represents a spectrum of symptoms that remain invisible to most clinicians, but identification would provide an improved approach to a treatment plan, additional patient understanding, and improved outcome.*
>
> —ROBERT DOBRIN, MD, FAAP, BEHAVIORAL PEDIATRICS AND CHILD/ADOLESCENT, ADULT PSYCHIATRY

This chapter deals with various types of head injuries, including traumatic brain injuries (TBI) and concussions. Regardless of the type of head injury, many individuals suffer with unrecognized lingering effects, some of which can be helped by wearing Irlen Spectral Filters. These individuals did not have these Irlen-like symptoms before their head injury; instead, the symptoms were the result of the injury. Yes, like other populations who acquired—rather than were born with—these symptoms, the Irlen Method has been proven to be able to eliminate many of these lingering symptoms.

Most people are not aware of the varied symptoms that can result from a head injury. Many individuals with some type of head injury suffer with:

- Difficulty with attention and concentration
- Headaches and/or other physical symptoms
- Light sensitivity
- Reading and learning problems

Because these conditions are not life-threatening, they are often over-looked by the professionals who diagnose, treat, and work with this population. This is sad because these symptoms can be improved or eliminated with the Irlen Method.

The second section of this chapter explains the tragic consequences of misdiagnosing Irlen symptoms, which can lead to individuals being identified with psychological problems. For those who have been misdiagnosed with psychological problems when they actually have Irlen Syndrome, the consequences can be dire.

An overview of the statistics related to brain injuries, concussions, and whiplash indicate that these are severe and significant problems for millions of children and adults. Over 1.5 million Americans suffer brain injuries each year that do not require hospitalization, and about the same number suffer concussions. Many more have severe head injuries requiring hospitalization and/or long-term rehabilitation. There are also 30,000 children diagnosed as having problems associated with TBI every year in the United States. Children who engage in various sports activities are prone to concussions, and sometimes repeated concussions, which have even more dire consequences. I have heard that the only "safe" sport might be ping pong. Head injuries, regardless of the type, are a serious concern for millions of children and adults.

People who sustain head injuries usually have to go to therapy to help with the recovery process. Initially, the focus of therapy is directed towards life-threatening conditions and healing the physical injuries. Other issues resulting from the head injury may not be recognized or addressed. However, it is often these very issues that may inhibit the individual's ability to return to school, work, adjust to daily living, or participate in social activities—it is also these issues that can be helped by the Irlen Method.

Statistics regarding the number of people who have sustained a brain injury, however, only tell part of the story, leaving out the countess millions who have mild concussions, showing no evidence of brain damage but continuing to live with unrecognized problems and silently suffering with no answers.

One drawback in the medical system is that diagnosing a head injury can be imprecise. Damage rarely shows up on CAT scans, MRIs, or other tests, resulting in individuals being told that they do not have a head injury when, in fact, they very well may. Lacking a definitive diagnosis, doctors may dismiss a patient's complaints of headaches, anxiety, dizziness, light sensitivity, or problems with reading, learning, or paying attention. Some individuals are simply told that such symptoms will lessen over time. Unfortunately, for many of these people, this is highly untrue. Finally, without a diagnosis, many individuals do not connect their symptoms to having had a head injury or concussion.

MAKING THE CONNECTION TO BRAIN INJURIES

Similar to those with medical and/or visual problems (discussed in Chapter 11), individuals who suffered from head injuries initially sought us out because they knew what reading was supposed to be like and how it had changed. These initial clients showed major improvements not just in reading, but many in other areas, when the Irlen Method was used. We, therefore, decided to conduct a study to determine the incidence of Irlen symptoms in the head injury population and whether these individuals would also experience the same improvements with Irlen Spectral Filters. Details about the study will be discussed in the following sections.

The First Client

The first person we saw who had a head injury was still dealing with severe cognitive, perceptual, reading, and other problems seven years after the injury occurred. Lucinda, as most clients with a severe head injury do, participated in years of various therapies including physical, occupational, and speech. She had made improvements; but not all of her problems were completely resolved. Lucinda knew that reading had never been a problem prior to her head injury. After researching her symptoms, she came across Irlen's website. She understood that she did not have Irlen Syndrome but realized that she had the same reading difficulties. However, typical of many individuals with a severe head injury, she was less aware of other problems that were also a result of the trauma to her brain. Also typical of many individuals who have sustained head injuries, she was so traumatized and overwhelmed by the change in her ability to function that she had only focused on a few of her symptoms, not all of them.

I recall clearly that when Lucinda, a woman in her mid-thirties, came into the office to be tested, she was using a walker. She had body tremors and seizure activity, was extremely light sensitive, and had trouble pulling her thoughts together to carry on a conversation, among a host of other difficulties. Even though she had been through multiple therapies in the seven years since her injury, she was still severely disabled;

unable to lead a normal life and barely able to participate in activities with her husband and young child. Her tremors made coordination so difficult that the simple act of picking up a glass and putting it in the dishwasher was so exhausting that she had to retire to her bed for the rest of the day. She explained that it took sheer will power and determination to do the simplest of tasks, and this left her exhausted. Even carrying on a conversation with others took too much effort, so she eventually gave up and stayed isolated in her house.

Being that she was the first person who came to see us because of a head injury, I asked her to make a list of all of her symptoms and keep a daily journal of which ones improved when she started wearing her Irlen Filters. I wanted to know which of her myriad of problems would be eliminated and how quickly they would disappear. This was the first time we were dealing with someone who had Irlen-like symptoms that were acquired as a result of an injury, and I was very curious to see the results.

Three Months Later

After three months, Lucinda came back to see me for her follow-up appointment. This time, she walked in without her walker. In fact, I didn't even recognize her at first. She looked completely different. She no longer suffered from tremors and no longer displayed any difficulty walking, talking, or carrying on the normal activities of life. She was smiling and carrying the journal she had kept for the past three months. As we talked, she told me that she actually reaches for her Irlen Filters and puts them on before she opens her eyes in the morning and gets out of bed. At night, she gets into bed and closes her eyes before taking them off, or she simply falls asleep with them on. She never wants to be without them and has even been known to wear them when taking a shower.

She then read the list of problems she had been tracking in her journal. I was not sure what to expect but was pleasantly surprised to learn that the positive changes she had experienced with her Irlen Filters had been almost immediate. Her reading abilities had improved, along with her sensitivity to light, depth perception, and her ability to pull her thoughts together and communicate. She no longer had headaches. Minor tasks that she had been having difficulty with, such as picking up and putting down objects and using a calculator, were beginning to come more easily to her.

I asked her if she would take the Irlen Filters off, so we would be able to see if the symptoms returned. She agreed, not knowing what to expect after wearing her Irlen Filters nonstop for three months. The change was almost immediate. Less than a minute after removing her filters, she began having tremors. She also got a headache, felt nauseous, couldn't think or pull her thoughts together, and had difficulty picking up a cup. The speed and severity by which all, not just some, of her symptoms returned took us both by surprise. The negative changes caused her to break down in tears because she had forgotten how difficult life had been the past seven years since her accident.

Continuing the Pattern

Not long after we treated our first traumatic brain injury client, a lawyer who also had a severe head injury (and was basically bedridden for the six months before seeing us) came in. She also was asked to keep a journal documenting the areas which improved, tracking how much the improvement occurred, and how soon. After she had been wearing her Irlen Filters for a few months, she returned. We shared a discussion similar to the one I had with the first head injury client, where she gleefully reported how her life had improved. Then I asked her to remove her Irlen Filters. When she did, she too immediately became overwhelmed and burst into tears as her symptoms returned.

Doing the Research

After seeing such dramatic changes with a few individuals, we decided to conduct a study at a southern California cognitive retraining program with fifty-five adults. Each individual in the program completed the self-test for Irlen Syndrome. The results showed that 69 percent of the group (thirty-eight adults) were suffering from light-based sensitivities, symptoms of physical discomfort, and perceptual difficulties, therefore making them suitable candidates for the Irlen Method. This proportion is substantially greater than the approximate 12 to 14 percent of the general population suffering from light sensitivity and perceptual processing difficulties. These participants were tested and, if appropriate, provided with their own unique Irlen Filters to wear. They were also asked to keep daily journals.

In reviewing each of the journals after a few months, we found the same patterns of improvement for a wide number of problems typically associated with a traumatic brain injury, such as motor coordination, body tremors, seizure activity, word retrieval, communication ability, attention difficulties, and reading problems. Some of these areas of improvement were familiar and considered Irlen-like symptoms, but other areas of improvement were new and exciting. Additionally, the journals revealed that these participants experienced a significant reduction in light sensitivity, headaches, fatigue, anxiety, and irritability with their Irlen Filters. Similar to the other brain injury clients we had treated, most of the changes occurred within a very short period of time.

The study showed that Irlen Filters were a successful intervention that could reduce sensory overload, allowing the brain to function in a more normal manner.

The individuals who participated in the study did not all have brain injuries that were caused by the same source. Some were stroke victims, while others sustained their injuries as a result of a car accident or beating. Additionally, multiple sclerosis, aneurysm, brain surgery, and seizure sufferers participated in the study. Regardless of the type of head injury, they all responded with the same positive changes as other populations mentioned in the book. This proved, once again, that it doesn't make a difference whether symptoms are inherited or acquired: Irlen Filters can make a difference.

Brain Surgery

While surgery has been life-saving for patients, it can sometimes result in neurological changes that can affect the individual's life.

Elizabeth, who had a brain tumor removed, sought out the Irlen Institute because after her surgery, she could no longer multitask. She went from being an outstanding reader to finding it extremely difficult to read. She had problems thinking, pulling her thoughts together, and communicating. Life, in general, had become very frustrating. Elizabeth rarely got headaches before the surgery, but afterward, reading, watching television, or working on the computer gave her headaches. In addition, she often spoke about sensory overload. "I shut down and just cannot think and function when in malls, stadiums, supermarkets, or other places with lots of fluorescent lights," she told us.

Like other clients with brain injuries, Elizabeth came to see us because her research showed her that the symptoms she was experiencing mirrored those of Irlen Syndrome. Screening showed that Elizabeth would benefit from the Irlen Method, and she was tested. She was then provided with her own uniquely colored Irlen Filters. Like they had for those who suffered from brain injuries, the filters made a huge difference by eliminating the Irlen-like symptoms.

Most often, people come to see us between six months and six years after their head injury or brain surgery. Typically, by the time they are screened and tested, they have had years of therapies and treatments and are left with some areas in which they have little hope for greater improvement. Like the other chapters have mentioned, the Irlen Method addresses symptoms that other therapies cannot address. However, only a certain percentage who have these symptoms will be helped by the Irlen Method. Having seen the results, we now encourage anyone who is experiencing the physical effects of head injuries—including concussions and whiplash—or other types of insults to the brain to take the self-tests on the Irlen Institute's website (www.irlen.com) to find out if the Irlen Method is an option for them.

IRLEN SYNDROME AND PSYCHOLOGICAL DISORDERS

For me, the Irlen Filters work wonders by toning down the visual screaming so that I can read, write, comprehend, and see whole pictures, not just pieces. So if you try and cure me with psychotherapy and we never get around to my piecemeal perception, of course my progress will be painfully slow or nonexistent. I may, in fact, get worse from the lifelong frustration of living with an invisible, overlooked, but gravely disabling perceptual defect that I was not even aware of as abnormal.

Now I know that none of this is my fault, my parents' fault, or anyone's fault. It's caused by how my brain perceives things, and I am relieved to finally know that I'm not acting nuts, and that the signals of danger are really false messages that my eyes are sending to my brain.

—NICK, IRLEN CLIENT FILES

There are many reasons why depression, panic disorders, conduct disorders, anxiety, and other psychological problems occur. Such issues may stem from a variety of causes, such as trauma, the result of physical abuse, or a chemical imbalance. However, in some cases, the environment can be an underlying cause. If lighting, visual activities, and other environmental conditions are causing sensory overload, this will result in changes in brain chemistry and biochemistry. These changes in how the brain functions can radically alter the way a person thinks, feels, and performs. They can even impair a person's range of neurological functions and—like any type of chronic stress—compromise the immune system. It is often difficult for the individual, and even the professional, to identify this type of problem as being the underlying issue, especially since there is no objective standard by which to judge "normal" perception.

For example, when an individual is in the midst of exploring the causes of the symptoms associated with mental issues (such as depression and feeling lethargic), rarely will a therapist ask about the effects of lighting, which most individuals sit underneath every day in school or the office. However, lighting is an environmental factor that needs to be considered, and there are many instances where the environment is what is causing the client's stress.

Psychological problems should be initially addressed with therapy and/or medication from mental health experts, but you will need to be aware that the environment can be contributing to your difficulties or possibly that you have been misdiagnosed.

Diagnosis at a Young Age

A growing number of children are being diagnosed at younger ages with psychological problems including depression, anxiety disorders, and bipolar disorder. This has resulted in increasing numbers of children in elementary schools taking mood-altering drugs that have never been tested on children and may have side effects. Like AD/HD, this may be the latest fad driven by new drugs, anxious parents, broad definitions, and more willingness on the part of the medical profession to medicate. This raises the question whether the increase is related to an increased awareness of early childhood psychological disorders or whether, tragically, many children are being misdiagnosed. This is an important difference because when psychological disorders are not due to a chemical imbalance, medication can result in side effects rather than being helpful.

Elementary school students are being diagnosed with depression and are being medicated. Often, there is something more to their so-called "depression" that is not being addressed, as is the case when a child is misdiagnosed. What appears as depression can come from a variety of sources, including diet, physical illnesses, learning problems, academic difficulties, and/or perceptual problems such as Irlen Syndrome.

Some misdiagnosed students, such as Belinda and Mark (whose stories follow), are fortunate enough to have parents who continued to seek out answers. If the medication prescribed to you or your child seemingly has no effect, do not stop questioning and searching for answers until you are satisfied with the results.

Belinda is in the second grade. When she was in first grade, she started complaining of headaches, stomachaches, and seeing things upside down and backwards. She was diagnosed with situational depression, was medicated, and was referred to a therapist. Unfortunately, none of the measures taken—medicinal or therapeutic—seemed to help.

Eventually, Belinda's parents came across the Irlen Method. They brought Belinda in for a consultation, and she has now been wearing her Irlen Filters for only a few months and is no longer having headaches or stomachaches. She no longer asks to go to the nurse's office in school at least three times a week complaining of not feeling well. She is happy, easily able to focus, gets her work done, and is no longer diagnosed as depressed.

—BELINDA, IRLEN CLIENT FILES

Mark was in sixth grade when his parents brought him to see me.

Although in special education classes, Mark was getting straight Fs. He was not working in class or doing his homework. He appeared depressed and even talked of suicide. The school blamed his parents, saying they were not spending enough time working with him.

In school, Mark's stomach and head hurt all the time. He could not listen or do his work, so he would put his head down on the desk and close his eyes. After school, he would go home and go to bed. After seeing a psychiatrist, Mark was labeled as depressed. Sharing her concerns with another parent whose child had had similar difficulties, Mark's mother found out that the Irlen Method had been helpful. Mark's mother immediately brought him to be tested, hoping that this was also his problem.

Mark's mother reports that with his favorite colored overlay, his reading immediately jumped from a second grade level to a sixth grade level. Wearing his Irlen Spectral Filters, Mark discovered the joy of not feeling sick. Needless to say, his mother reports that he is a different child, happy and confident.

—MARK, IRLEN CLIENT FILES

Rod, however, was not as lucky as Belinda or Mark. He was not diagnosed with Irlen Syndrome until he was thirty-three. By that time, according to his family, "life had become too painful," and not knowing what else to do, Rod committed suicide.

The following quotation is paraphrased from Rod's book, *Undiagnosed Up Until Now:*

> *Being diagnosed with Irlen gives me an explanation for why I was so disoriented most of the time, why my brain was working overtime to make sense of things, why I was confused, unable to concentrate, frustrated, anxious, fatigued, depressed, and could not achieve what everyone else could. My life is an ongoing struggle, and I feel like a salmon swimming upstream against the flow. I am always bashing my head against a brick wall.*

According to his mother, wearing Irlen Filters helped Rod very much in the six months that he had them. However, years of living with immense chronic pain, experiencing constant anxiety, and panic attacks had taken a severe toll on his mind and body; and he felt completely depleted by the time he was diagnosed with Irlen Syndrome. In his book, Rod expresses his frustration that no one had recognized or addressed his Irlen symptoms. Also paraphrased from Rod's book:

> *I don't see what you see. It's all going too fast and seems unreal to me. Wouldn't it be better if I could see nothing? The world is whirling, the words are swirling, the lights are blinding, and my head is full of pain. Somebody help me, can you understand?*

For information on how to order Rod's book, see page 198.

Rod's very painful story will hopefully serve as a reminder of how important it is not to wait or settle when there is an issue or a problem that you see in your children or in yourself. Immediately seek treatment; and if you are not satisfied with the results, do not stop searching for other options until you find one that works. As in Rod's case, being misdiagnosed and only treated for a psychological disorder can result in tragic endings.

Misdiagnosis

Much of what was discussed in previous chapters, such as illnesses, diseases and other sources of discomfort, are not direct results of Irlen Syndrome but are rather issues that have mirroring symptoms (that can, often enough, be treated by the Irlen Method).

Of course, disorders such as agoraphobia, anxiety, depression, and panic attacks can be caused by a chemical imbalance and treated with medication and/or therapy. However, those same psychological disorders can be misdiagnosed and really be a result of Irlen Syndrome, not a chemical imbalance. We have helped individuals who have been misdiagnosed with the following psychological conditions.

Agoraphobia

Agoraphobia is an anxiety disorder where people often avoid going places; and, in many cases, they very rarely leave their homes.[1] Agoraphobia is real but can be misdiagnosed. I have two clients in the same family who spent years never leaving their rooms. Finally, as adolescents, they came to see me. Their bedrooms, which they refused to leave, were so dark that they were like caves. Lighting, any lighting, made them feel incredibly sick, nauseous, and terribly anxious. Therefore, they avoided being in light, which regrettably meant staying in their dark bedrooms. Their Irlen Spectral Filters eliminated all of their physical symptoms triggered by light, and, as a result, they are no longer frightened of leaving their rooms and getting sick. They now lead normal and productive lives. What appeared to be agorapbobia had been brought on by symptoms of Irlen Syndrome.

Conduct Disorder

Sometimes, the stress of holding it together all day will cause a child to have an outburst at home, especially when asked to do homework. The child may scream, yell, or hit inanimate objects. It would be wrong to assume that this child is bipolar or has conduct disorder, when, in fact, she has undiagnosed reading and learning problems related to Irlen Syndrome. Sadly, since the cause of the stress is not being identified or addressed, the stress just builds up all over again and the cycle continues.

Depression

Depression can come from many sources, including undiagnosed Irlen Syndrome. Over the years, I have helped many children who became sick, tired, or fatigued under fluorescent lighting and/or could not keep up academically and were misdiagnosed with depression. These children would protect themselves from the lighting, using behaviors such as putting their heads down on their desks, covering their heads, refusing to do their schoolwork, or spending lots of time sleeping instead of playing with their friends. These students may be bright, but they are unable to reach their full potential.

I worked with one "depressed" teenager whose psychiatrist wanted him to take medication, but the teen's mom did not believe he was depressed. Even though he appeared depressed at school and came home and slept, he would wake up and have all kinds of energy at night. According to his mother, her son was a totally different child when it was dark.

"It didn't correlate; why he would he be depressed only during the daytime and wake up at night," she said. She also noticed that he kept his room completely dark, with the blinds always closed and the walls painted black. His behavior was inconsistent. Determined to help her son, his mother searched the internet for "light sensitivity" and related issues. Eventually, she came across Irlen Syndrome and took her son in for testing. He now wears Irlen Filters and is a different child. Remember, it's important that as an advocate for your child, you look for clues and do not just take labels at face value.

There are situations where depression actually does develop from the frustration of living with an undiagnosed perceptual disorder. This situation usually occurs with students who are intelligent but frustrated because they cannot achieve. These students struggle but cannot keep up, blame themselves for not succeeding, and feel a sense of hopelessness because they do not know how to change things and do better. They despair over their poor achievement and, as adults, agonize over not being able to achieve their dreams. I have seen children and adults who are depressed because they cannot keep up with their schoolwork, cannot achieve good grades, or they struggle in their careers and cannot figure out why it is so hard for them, especially when they know they are smart. They never realized that they had Irlen Syndrome.

One of my clients, Susan, falls into this category. She was nineteen years old and had dropped out of college when she first came to see me. High school had been very difficult for her—she worked very hard but could only manage to get Cs. She had been seeing a psychiatrist since the fourth grade, as well as a behavior therapist for anger management. In addition to *Adderall* for ADD, Susan was placed on lithium and *Lametal* for depression after dropping out of college.

After talking with Susan, I discovered that lighting—especially fluorescent lights—caused her to feel dizzy, anxious, irritable, and unable to focus or listen. Reading was exceptionally painful, and she had to stop after a few pages because she became dizzy and sick. She qualified for Irlen Filters, and with her Irlen Filters, Susan was able to return to college and succeed.

In Susan's case, her misdiagnosis of ADD and depression were a result of her Irlen Syndrome going undiagnosed for so long.

Panic Attacks and Anxiety

People with panic disorders struggle with sudden, discrete periods of intense anxiety, mounting physiological arousal, fear, stomach problems, overwhelming feelings of terror, and intense physical symptoms.

Many individuals with Irlen Syndrome experience anxiety and frequent panic attacks due to the constantly changing distortions that are a part of the syndrome.

> *At forty-one years of age, Lucy was diagnosed with anxiety disorder. She tried medications, many different therapies, diet change, and took classes to learn to manage her anxiety. If she was in a grocery store for more than five minutes, she would have a panic attack. She kept saying that there was "too much going on," but she did not have the other common panic disorder symptoms of a racing heart, shortness of breath, or the shakes. She just felt visually overwhelmed, couldn't find anything she was looking for, and had to leave the store. Now, with her Irlen Filters, she no longer gets overwhelmed and can shop for as long as she wants.*

—LUCY, IRLEN CLIENT FILES

CONCLUSION

The goal of this chapter and the previous chapter is to illustrate the fact that that while head injuries, medical conditions, and psychological problems need to be professionally treated by medical and mental health experts, medication and therapies may not always solve the issue. This can be for a variety of reasons, including a misdiagnosis. The bottom line is, the Irlen Method can be an intervention that eliminates some of the debilitating symptoms.

Many of the individuals we have treated for Irlen Syndrome have a similar profile to the individual described in the previous paragraph. They prefer evenings when they feel better and are more alive, alert, attentive, and productive.

Brain injuries and psychological disorders make some people more susceptible to their environment, resulting in severe physical symptoms and perceptual distortions. Irlen Filters can normalize brain chemistry, biochemistry, help the neurological system function better, and protect the immune system. As a result, despite injuries and psychological issues, a person can feel better, have more energy, and be able to lead a more active life.

Conclusion

Since writing my last book, *Reading by the Colors,* more and more people have been seeking out the Irlen Method, asking, "Even if I don't have Irlen Syndrome, can I still be helped?" As you have learned from the preceding chapters, the answer is often yes. Our understanding of perceptual processing problems, their symptoms, and how they affect individuals has grown significantly since my first book was published. We have seen the Irlen Method evolve from helping an initial group of thirty-five adults to changing the lives of hundreds of thousands of people with Irlen Syndrome or acquired Irlen-like symptoms, stemming from a wide variety of different diagnoses including illnesses, disorders, and even head injuries. I hope that this book has created awareness of the problems so many individuals face and that it has presented one—or many—possible solutions.

Of course, the first step for the individual is realizing that what he is experiencing is not "normal." It is with this awareness that he can choose to seek out the proper solution and make a change. Of course, many times it is children who are affected by Irlen Syndrome; children who have grown up with Irlen and therefore do not know that life can be different. For these children, it is up to the parents to recognize that something is wrong before the child is misdiagnosed or dismissed. Many times, parents are able to identify something in themselves that will lead to clues about their child's difficulties. Use the questions asked in each chapter to determine if certain behaviors may be your child's way of telling you that there is a problem or a way of compensating. Pay attention and ask the questions posed throughout the book to see if you or your child is indeed suffering with Irlen symptoms, then act sooner rather than later. Too many people do nothing for too long while their children continue to suffer.

The majority of this book creates awareness of various types of problems that can result from light sensitivity, physical symptoms, and perceptual distortions. It is very important to stress that perceptual processing difficulties are not the only roadblock and that Irlen Spectral Filters are not the only solution to consider. The Irlen Method is only a piece of the puzzle, and I hope that this book gives you the information you need to be able to identify both Irlen symptoms as well as other pieces of the puzzle.

Most significantly, the stories throughout each chapter illustrate how important it is to be a good detective. Otherwise, it is easy to misdiagnose, mislabel, and as a result, provide treatment that will not address Irlen symptoms.

For many people, a misdiagnosis can be equated to being in the right house but on the wrong floor. How can you change if you are not addressing the correct problem? Visual processing is a complex problem. The brain is constantly being bombarded with visual information that has been dissected into millions of signals, each being processed separately and finally put back together into the picture you see. Many things can cause the system to break down so that the brain can no longer filter visual information properly.

Additionally, people differ greatly in how they respond to their environment—and those with Irlen Syndrome have an inherited predisposition to environmental stress. Most people have brains that can filter incoming stimuli so that dealing with the environment is not particularly overwhelming. But for those with Irlen symptoms—whether they are inherited or acquired—the visual information is not appropriately filtered. The brain becomes disorganized and chaotic trying to deal with the constant flow of sensory information. When the brain is struggling to process visual information, this affects so many other parts of the body, causing biochemical changes, physical symptoms, and distorted perception which changes how we think, feel, and function. Health, learning, and performance can be compromised by factors of lighting, glare, contrast, and the need to read and pay attention for long periods at a time.

While writing this book, it was also my hope to promote awareness, education, and the idea of continuing to seek a solution to perceptual processing problems. It is imperative that you do not let the first diagnosis you receive dictate the course of treatment—for yourself or your child—unless you are absolutely sure that it is correct. As discussed in the book, a misdiagnosis in regard to learning and reading problems, AD/HD, dyslexia, and/or other issues is not at all uncommon in a culture that looks for one-size-fits-all cures through medication, remediation, and learning through repetition. Conditions like perceptual processing disorders are not easily identified through testing, and therefore they are often overlooked, which can result in an incomplete or misdiagnosis. This can be very misleading and potentially damaging to yourself or your child, who may end up on unnecessary medication with possible side effects.

As a parent, remember, you know your child better than anyone else; so you need to keep on searching for the solution if symptoms persist. That is one of the main themes I hope you will take away with you from this book—do not give up. The stories within each chapter illustrate how numerous parents and educators refused to give up in their search for the solution to a child's symptoms, many of which are physical and painful. Just like these parents and educators, you need to not accept that something will "simply go away" or that someone "will have these symptoms for the rest of their life." The one comment I have heard over and over again is, "The Irlen Method not only improved my reading, it changed my life." I'm not talking about curing an illness, but rather, making symptoms disappear. Eliminating the barriers that prevent your child or yourself from having a better life is what the Irlen Method is all about. It should be your mission as well.

To learn more about Helen Irlen and the Irlen Method, visit the Irlen Institute's website at www.irlen.com.

APPENDIX A

Additional Causes of Learning Difficulties and Recommendations for Treatment

Irlen Syndrome is only a piece of the puzzle, and the Irlen Method can help only certain individuals. Therefore, this Appendix describes other underlying and silent root causes for difficulties in attention, concentration, and performance. Additionally, it provides a variety of recommendations to help these issues. Because the medical profession doesn't usually connect unexplained symptoms such as fatigue, headaches, dizziness, and stomachaches with learning difficulties, these symptoms are often ignored. Therefore, these are the symptoms that you, as a parent, need to be on the lookout for.

Included in this Appendix are a variety of different conditions—all of which may be accompanied by physical symptoms—and recommendations for you to follow to help alleviate these symptoms. These problems run in families and are usually inherited. If you, or another family member, have any of these problems, be sure to watch your child extra carefully to see if you can determine the cause of the problem. Once you have figured it out, you should consider trying one or more of the suggestions in this Appendix. Sometimes, even a small change can make a big difference. Be alert. When your child does not feel well, it impacts upon attention, learning, and performance.

Allergies

If your child has allergies, check to make sure that he does not feel tired, sleepy, hyperactive, inattentive, or sick when his allergies are acting up during the school day.

There are some things you can try to make sure that physical symptoms do not interfere with learning and performance.

- Alternative therapies. Some parents prefer alternative medicine and have found treatment by naturopathic and holistic practitioners and/or alternative medicine providers, such as acupuncturists or chiropractors, helpful.

- Consult a professional. Consult your pediatrician or an allergist for an evaluation. This can lead to treatment to control the symptoms.

- Educate. If problems persist, inform your child's teacher about the ongoing issues. Additionally, educate your child to take responsibility for reporting these symptoms to the teacher.

- Interventions and accommodations. Certain classroom interventions and modifications can be implemented. For example, tape recording classroom lectures, reducing the assignment load, allowing additional time for assignments and tests, dividing up tests into sections with breaks, or administering part of the test in the morning and part of the test in the afternoon are all possible solutions. However, you will likely need to discuss these accommodations with your child's classroom teacher or principal.

- Over-the-counter medication. Some individuals find over-the-counter products to be helpful, but consult with your doctor first.

- Research your child's allergy medication. Make sure the allergy medication he is taking is not causing physical symptoms. If your child's symptoms are listed as potential side effects of the medication, determine whether the symptoms outweigh the benefits or ask your pediatrician to provide an alternative medication.

Antibiotic Use

Ear and other infections, which have necessitated the frequent use of antibiotics over a number of years, can result in intestinal yeast overgrowth. This can impair the immune system and increase the likelihood of additional infections and additional antibiotic usage.

The following are recommendations that may address this problem.

- Consult a professional. Consult a nutritionist, allergist, or investigate natural remedies available at health food stores regarding help for long-term effects of chronic antibiotic use.

- Don't take antibiotics alone. Using Acidophilus or eating yogurt with any further use of antibiotics is recommended. Acidophilus is a probiotic that contains certain good bacteria that helps counter the negative affects of antibiotics.

- Get tested. Some professionals believe that the steady use of antibiotics can contribute to the body's ability to absorb nutrients, affecting the immune system. For more information on this problem and recommended testing, refer to www.greatplainslaboratory.com or other websites on the internet.

- Try dietary supplements. Custom Probiotics, Inc., is a company that formulates and supplies custom blends of very high bacterial count, multiple-strain Acidophilus and Bifidus dietary supplements. For more information, go to www.customprobiotics.com.

Eating Patterns

Some individuals experience physical symptoms when they are unable to eat between meals. These symptoms can include feeling sick or dizzy; getting headaches or stomachaches; being tired; or feeling shaky, grumpy, irritable, or distracted, which can affect school performance, attention, and behavior. You do not have to have a medical diagnosis to benefit from the following recommendations.

- Eat by the clock. Eat regularly, approximately every two hours, rather than waiting until you are hungry. Do not use your body to tell you when to eat.

- Eat small meals. In some cases, eating small meals more frequently (as opposed to three larger meals) can help eliminate symptoms some people experience from not eating often enough. Consult a doctor or dietician about the advisability of eating small meals more frequently. In some European countries, it is more common to eat several small meals than a couple of very large meals in the course of a day.

- Educate. Educate your child about these different options. Have your child take responsibility for his own health and dietary needs.

- Plan for tests. Examinations can be very stressful for children, and stressing can cause a drop in blood sugar. This can make it difficult to maintain concentration and perform adequately. Speak with your student's teacher about allowing your child to bring either nutritious snacks or a protein drink to long examinations and day-long tests.

- Snack throughout the day. It is a good idea to eat small, nutritious protein snacks throughout the day in addition to three meals (another option would be to eat numerous small meals—see the second bullet on this list). For example, some people (children and adults) may prefer to have a bag of nuts or a smoothie at their desk to snack on during the day. When planning your child's meals, you might also incorporate snacks of cheese or another protein drink for him to snack on between meals. If necessary, discuss the situation with your child's teacher or the school principal.

- Supplement with fish oil. You may want to increase brain power with fish oil. Many individuals with learning and attention problems have found fish oil supplements to be helpful. When buying, remember to get pure fish oil supplement

- Try increasing protein. Have protein at each meal and for snacks. You can eat protein snacks or have smoothies or protein shakes.

Food Sensitivities

Food sensitivities are far more common than most people realize and result in a variety of physical symptoms. Many different foods, not just sugar, can cause problems. Headaches, congestion, fatigue, dizziness, stomachaches, hyperactivity, irritability, shakiness, or moodiness can all result from a food sensitivity and affect classroom attention, performance, and behavior.

To find out if your child has food sensitivities, which foods are causing a problem, and how to help alleviate these physical symptoms, follow the suggestions in this section.

- Get tested. Consult your physician for recommendations. There are laboratories that test for metabolic problems by using blood samples to conduct urine organic tests, immune deficiency panels, basic allergy tests, and tests for gluten and casein antibodies.

- Keep a journal. If your child experiences physical symptoms after eating but you do not know which foods or beverages may be causing the problem, keep a journal. Ask your child to tell you if his head or stomach bothers him after eating. Note any behavior changes, such as hyperactivity or fatigue after eating. Write down everything your child eats and drinks and also keep track of his symptoms and when they occur. If you start to notice a pattern, such as certain symptoms always occurring after specific foods, there is a good chance that your child has a sensitivity to that particular food or beverage. Food cravings can also indicate a food sensitivity.

- Read books on food allergies and special diets. *Special Diets for Special Kids* by Lisa Lewis is a great example. In her book, Lewis helps parents understand and implement special diets that can be beneficial to children with autism and related developmental disorders. Additionally, *Food Allergy Relief* by Dr. James Braly (with Jim Thompson) is a great read. Learn about the nature of food allergies, related diseases, and natural therapies and treatments. Finally, *Feast Without Yeast* by Bruce Sermon and Lori Kornblu teaches that too much yeast can result in headaches, fatigue, depression, and other symptoms that overlap with symptoms of Irlen Syndrome. The book also includes numerous yeast-free recipes.

- See a specialist. You may want to consult your physician, allergist, dietician, or nutritionist regarding the best type of balanced diet to reduce symptoms.

- Try an elimination diet. It is important, if you suspect your child is sensitive to a specific food, to eliminate that food completely from his diet. This will allow you to make sure that there are not other foods that are causing problems. It will take at least three weeks for the offending food(s) to be out of the system completely, so chances are you may not see improvements until after this time period. Your child's behavior may get worse before it gets better because the body tends to crave the food it is sensitive to—especially if the specific food has been eliminated.

- Visit websites on food additives and related testing. Some good examples are www.fedupwithfoodadditives.info, a comprehensive website that explains food additives and their impact upon your well-being and that of your children; and www.feingold.org, which presents details on the Feingold diet. Food dyes, additives, and preservatives can cause physical symptoms affecting performance.

Noise Sensitivities

Some individuals are bothered by loud noises or a lot of noise, making it difficult to focus or concentrate. People with noise sensitivities may cover their ears in class, on the playground, or in movie theaters.

The following solutions may prove to be instrumental for someone with noise sensitivities.

- Changing seats. Moving away from the offending noise or choosing a seat that is not near windows or open doors can help eliminate excess noise. If your child's classroom has assigned seating, discuss this option with his teacher or principal.

- iPod. White noise in the form of soft music helps some individuals concentrate in noisy environments. It should not be too loud!

- Soft ear plugs. People with noise sensitivities can carry soft ear plugs at all times so they can use them whenever necessary. This muffles the sound so it is more tolerable, but the student will still be able to hear his teacher.

- Sound therapy. There are different therapies that have been found to be beneficial for some people who suffer noise sensitivities. Some of these therapies include biowaves or sound therapy, both of which reduce sensitivity to noise.

Sleep Patterns

There are two types of sleep patterns that need to be recognized and addressed for peak performance—the "night owl" sleep pattern and the "early bird" sleep pattern. Night owls have difficulty going to sleep and waking up. Generally, night owls experience difficulties attending, concentrating on, and performing in morning classes. Early birds, on the other hand, tend to be early risers who get tired at night.

The following suggestions are for night owls who need help being alert in the morning.

- Consider career choices. Those who follow a night owl sleep pattern do not conform well to the typical 9 AM to 5 PM workday. These people should investigate careers that have flexible hours, allow telecommuting, or offer afternoon/evening work hours.

- Exercising. Exercising first thing in the morning can be helpful in promoting attending behavior and increasing energy level. Have your child try running, walking, or any other type of exercise before his classes begin.

- Homework. Allow your child to take a break after school before starting homework.

- Record classes. In high school, your child may find it helpful to tape early morning classes so that the information can be reviewed later at home, with fewer distractions. You may need to ask for permission from the teacher to tape the class.

- Scheduling classes. Suggest that your child schedule more academically demanding classes, such as reading, math, science and/or social studies classes, later in the day if at all possible. If necessary, speak with your child's guidance counselor about the issue. For college students, scheduling all classes after 10 AM is a good idea.

- Shower in the morning. Taking a shower in the morning rather than at night can help wake a child up at the right time.

- Studying. Night owls benefit more from staying up late to study rather than waking up early to finish studying or complete homework.

For early birds, strategies opposite to ones night owls should try will likely be successful.

- Homework. Early birds do better completing work in the morning before school rather than staying up late to finish assignments.

- Studying. Early birds do better getting up early to finish studying rather than trying to cram all their studying in at night.

- Scheduling classes. Early birds do better taking day rather than evening classes, since they are too tired to concentrate in the evening.

Smell Sensitivities

For some individuals, certain strong smells can result in headaches, stomachaches, or simply a sick feeling. Dry erase markers, sharpies, detergents, perfumes, colognes, and hair spray are common triggers for these sensitivities. Symptoms that result from these sensitivities can interfere with a child's ability to learn and stay focused in the classroom. However, there are some things you can do to help ensure your child is not subjected to smells that will make him feel ill.

- Change your child's seat. If dry erase markers cause headaches or stomachaches, make sure your child does not sit next to the whiteboards. If there is assigned seating, discuss the possibility of moving his seat with the teacher.

- Use unscented markers. Give your child unscented markers for him to use at school.

- Self-advocacy. Teach your child to let you and the teacher know when certain smells cause physical symptoms. Helping your child develop self-advocacy skills is important to be able to let teachers know when there is an issue. Hopefully, this will allow your child to be able to move away from scents that are bothersome. You can always send an initial note to the teacher, but teaching your child to speak up is important.

Thyroid Problems

Thyroid problems can be inherited and run in families, and they can cause a wide variety of symptoms including headaches, migraines, and fatigue, all of which can lead to difficulty focusing, concentrating, and performing in school. If someone in your family had thyroid problems, or if you think your child is displaying symptoms of a thyroid problem, the following options should prove to be beneficial when trying to remedy the issue.

- Consult. Consult your physician and mention your family history. The physician will likely ask a few questions and help you determine the next step to take.

- Get tested. If there is a family history of thyroid problems, periodic testing is suggested. Thyroid problems can appear in adolescence or possibly in the 20s or 30s. Thyroid testing is generally not invasive and usually consists of a simple blood test to determine thyroid levels.

APPENDIX B

Strategies for Dealing With Academic Problems

Although Irlen Syndrome can contribute to academic difficulties, some-times neither the Irlen Method nor any other method can remove the learning barrier. In recognition of the many other pieces of the puzzle, and also wanting to provide your child with the greatest likelihood for success, this Appendix includes strategies for success. It is full of suggestions for the struggling learner. For learning strategies to be helpful, they must match the student's individual learning style.

This Appendix provides a variety of different strategies for each of the areas needed for academic success. These strategies can easily be implemented in the classroom because they do not require additional teacher time or money. Determine the areas in which your child is struggling first and then try the different suggested strategies for success. Find the perfect fit for your child.

The type of learning strategies that are useful can vary as your child advances in the school system and different competencies are required. Therefore, re-evaluate these strategies yearly because they may need to be changed or different ones added. For some students, academic success may be a combination of skill building and successfully incorporating learning strategies.

LISTENING/ATTENTION PROBLEMS

One area students experience problems with in school is in listening and paying attention. Your child may be inattentive, easily distracted, have difficulty following direction, misinterpret verbal information, or need material repeated. Class notes may be incomplete because she has a difficulty listening and taking notes simultaneously. Determine if any of the following suggestions would be helpful. You may need to discuss some of the following options with your child's teacher.

- Looking away. Some individuals have trouble looking and listening simultaneously. Teachers need to understand that these students are not being inattentive or rude. These students are better able to concentrate and retain verbal information when not looking at the speaker. This blocks out the interfering visual clues. To an unknowing teacher, it may seem like a child is not paying attention. Discuss this tactic with your child's teacher.

- Motor activity. Some students find that it is easier to attend and stay on task when engaged in some type of motor activity, such as drawing or manipulating items like pencils, squeeze balls, or soft squishy objects. Talk to your child's teacher to make sure it is okay for your child to bring one of these objects to class.

- Preferential seating. Request that your child is seated towards the front of the room, close to the teacher.

- Soft ear plugs. These can be effective in reducing the noise level in the classroom, which can be distracting when taking tests, reading, or studying.

- Sound enhancer. Try implementing a wireless microphone system or have your child cup one or both hands behind her ears when listening to lectures. This can make the speaker's voice sound louder, which helps to reduce distraction and increase your child's attention.

- Tape recorder. Have your child tape lectures with a variable speed recorder that has a counter. Playing the information at a slightly faster speed will cut the listening time, while still allowing your child to replay information as needed. Keep an outline of the material—along with the corresponding number on the counter—so that your child is easily able to go back to a section and re-listen if necessary.

- Teacher's notes. Request that your child's teacher provides outlines or lecture notes on what will be discussed in class. Knowledge of the material and sequence in which the material will be covered can help with comprehension and retention.

MATH PROBLEMS

If your child has difficulty remembering math facts, formulas, or the order of the steps in division, multiplication, and other equations, calculations take longer. This often creates problems with accuracy and timed tests. Here are some suggestions.

- Color model. If your child has difficulty remembering the various math steps for multiplication and division, you can color code each math function differently, which may serve as a memory enhancer. Tape a card with a math problem on your child's desk as a model to refer to with the addition steps in one color, subtraction in another color, and multiplication and division steps in different colors.

- Finger math. Finger math is a way of doing addition and multiplication without using a calculator or multiplication tables. If you visit www.fingerithmatic.com, you and your child can learn how to do finger math. There are also finger math videos on www.metacafe.com (just type "finger math" into the search box).

- Graph paper. Try having your child write math problems on graph paper or have her turn her notebook paper horizontally to help with column alignment.

MEMORY PROBLEMS

For some children, retaining math facts, sight vocabulary, and spelling can be hard. Retention does not come easily, even with practice and repetition. Try the following memory-enhancing strategies to find which one matches your child's learning style.

- Physical movement. Spelling words and math facts are given different movements using writing in the air or in sand; cheerleading; or Tai Chi movements.

- Saying. Some students learn by saying rather than writing. While it does not work for everyone, writing something once and then using verbal repetition is effective for some.

- Singing. Putting math facts or spelling words to music makes them easier to remember.

- Visualization. Having your child associate words with pictures can be beneficial. For example, the words "hoping" and "hopping" can be easily confused. However, if your child learns to associate the single "p" in "hoping" with a heart and the double "pp" in "hopping" as two feet, it may help her to differentiate the two words and enhance her memory.

READING PROBLEMS

There are many factors aside from Irlen Syndrome that can contribute to reading difficulties, such as below grade level reading skills, comprehension issues, and difficulty with word recognition. The following suggestions do not substitute for reading instruction. However, they may provide your child with the ability to learn and keep up with her classmates while working on improving reading skills.

Below Grade Level Reading Skills

If your child cannot read grade level material, there are a few options you can try to guarantee that reading difficulties are not prohibiting her from learning.

- Discuss strategies with your child's school. See if another student (possibly in an older grade) can read textbooks to your child or read the textbook onto a tape so that your child can replay the material. Suggest to the school that extra credit be given to the reader.

- Inquire about textbooks on tape. Some schools offer textbooks on tape for the visually impaired. These books can also be provided to others who have reading difficulties. Additionally, books on tape are often also available at local libraries.

- Purchase a Readingpen. A Readingpen scans a word from any printed text. It displays the word in larger print. The word is read aloud from a built-in speaker or through earphones that can be attached to the Readingpen. The pen also defines the word. A single pen can be purchased for under $300. Visit www.readingpen.com for more information.

- Read to your child or read and tape. If you tape the material, your child can listen and repeat sections as necessary. However, reading to your child is also beneficial because then she can ask questions as you progress. You can also summarize and discuss the material.

Comprehension

If your child has trouble comprehending the material when reading, try the following strategies.

- Consider different styles of reading. Not every student comprehends by reading silently. Try reading aloud or reading aloud onto a tape and listening to it later with your child to determine which provides the best comprehension of the material.

- Highlight or outline the reading material.

- Practice identifying main ideas.

- Read topic sentences, introductions, and summaries before reading the material.

- Try paired reading. This is when you share the reading with your child. Your child reads a paragraph or page and then you read a paragraph or page while she follows along.

- Try the SQ3R reading method. SQ3R stands for Survey, Question, Read, Recite, and Review. First, scan the table of contents of the book. Second, as you begin each chapter, review section headings, pictures and graphs, and study guides or questions. Third, read the chapter and underline or highlight important items. Fourth, summarize or explain what you read. Finally, re-read and study the information that you underlined or highlighted.

Word Recognition

If your child has trouble recognizing words, there are a few different approaches that may be helpful. When reading with your child, try the following strategies.

- Look for smaller, familiar words within larger words.

- Place unfamiliar words on flashcards and review them with your child for both pronunciation and meaning.

- Scan the page(s) for unfamiliar words before reading. Review and rehearse these words with your child before reading.

- Sound out unfamiliar words.

- Think of words with similar sounds.

SPELLING PROBLEMS

Spelling problems can affect report writing, essays, note taking, copying, and test taking, resulting in lower grades on papers or having to redo papers. These difficulties can affect a student's ability to put her thoughts down on paper. When writing, some students have a tendency to think in one language and then reorganize their thoughts into words that they can spell. This can limit the quality and quantity of a written assignment.

The following strategies can help your child remember how to spell words correctly, since not all words can be spelled correctly by sounding them out.

- Color coding. You cannot always depend on sounding out words to spell them correctly, since in the English language words are not always spelled as they sound. To help children learn and retain the correct spelling of words, assign a different color to each vowel so the colors are consistently associated with the letter. This can help when studying for spelling tests with your child. Using words that your child is having difficulty spelling, write the word with the missed vowels in the assigned color. Use unassigned colors for other letters that are missed. Children then practice the word by looking at the color-coded word. They then close their eyes and picture the word, spelling it in their heads. It is easier to remember that the word has a green letter then a red letter versus whether it is spelled with "ae" or "ea."

- Misspeller's dictionary. A misspeller's dictionary includes words the way they are most likely to be misspelled. This allows the student to find a word the way she would spell it. For many, this dictionary is easier to use than a regular dictionary because if you cannot spell the word, it is impossible to look it up in a regular dictionary. Misspeller's dictionaries are available through Barnes and Noble (www.bn.com) or Amazon (www.amazon.com).

- Personal dictionary. Give your child an address book to use as a personalized, pocket-sized dictionary. Your child writes the words that she frequently uses but has difficulty spelling into the book under the correct letter. Once she reaches the upper grades, a personal dictionary can be created for each subject area and, with a teacher's permission, used while taking tests.

- Spelling units. There are many different types of portable electronic handheld spelling units, which allow the student to punch in a word and get the correct spelling. A few examples are the Spelling Tutor, the Franklin Speller, and the Franklin Talking Dictionary & Spell Corrector, which can be found either at school supply stores or at www.franklin.com.

- Thesaurus. Don't have your child look up words in a dictionary; instead, have her use a thesaurus or word lists. A thesaurus contains a list of words in alphabetical order for quick identification. It is easier to find words by scanning down a word list rather than trying to figure out how to spell the word in order to look it up in a dictionary.

HANDWRITING PROBLEMS

If your child avoids writing, writes as little as possible, writes very slowly, frequently makes errors while writing, or if her writing is slow and laborious, accommodations need to be considered. In some cases, a child's handwriting is neat, but it takes an effort to get it that way. For others, handwriting starts out neat but deteriorates as writing continues. For both of these situations, strategies should be considered.

You want to make sure that you look beyond neatness when determining if your child has a writing problem.

When the written process is not automatic and takes an effort, it can affect an individual's ability to successfully complete written tasks, put thoughts down on paper, copy accurately from a book or chalkboard, complete tests within time limits, take good notes, or learn material through copying. The school may not be aware that the child has a problem, especially if her handwriting is neat.

The following strategies can be of help if your child struggles with writing problems.

- Answers only. Instead of your child copying questions and math problems that need to be answered, have her write down answers only. This eliminates fatigue and avoidance of doing the assignments.

- Graph paper. Have your child use graph paper for writing math problems. This can improve column alignment and uniformity of letter size and spacing.

- Lined paper. Your child's handwriting may be improved by increasing or decreasing the size of the space between lines on paper or by using primary-size lined paper.

- Markers. If writing with pens or pencils is too difficult for your child, have her try using a marker, which takes less pressure and effort to write with.

- Mechanical pencils or pens. Mechanical pencils and pens (such as Dr. Grip) can increase the flow of your child's writing. They also require less effort to write with than standard pencils or pens.

- Note taking. Modify notes by either using phonetic approximations for words which cannot be spelled or creating shorthand and/or symbols for words.

- Oral spelling tests. If you notice a significant difference between the way your child performs on oral spelling tests and written spelling tests, request oral administration of spelling tests.

- Print work. If your child's cursive is sloppy, slow, laborious, deteriorates, or takes an effort to complete all assignments, print or type all work. If learning cursive is necessary see if the teacher can provide separate exercises to practice cursive writing.

- Soft pencil grip. If your child has an awkward pencil grip, this can cause writing problems and fatigue. Provide your child with a soft pencil grip, which slides on over the pencil, making writing easier and more comfortable. These can be purchased at pretty much any school or office supply store.

- Speak and write software. Naturally speaking software like Dragon NaturallySpeaking lets your child talk to the computer to complete essay assignments rather than actually write the essay. The student can simply speak, and the words appear on the screen.

- Tape record lectures. If your child is granted permission to tape lectures, have her use a variable speed tape recorder with a counter to play back the lectures in less time. Keep an outline of topics and the counter number of where each topic begins on the tape to make it easier to listen only to certain parts of the lecture.

- Unlined paper. If your child's writing is large so that it is difficult to keep the writing within the lines, try having her use unlined paper or primary-size lined paper to see if this makes it easier to write legibly.

- Write it once. Minimize the use of written repetition to enhance learning. Instead, use oral repetition, visualization, or a tactile approach to help your child learn material.

- Write letters on colored cards. This tactic can be very helpful for letter reversals, such as confusing b and d or m and w. Write one set of letters on each card—capital and lowercase, such as "D d" on one card and "B b" on another one, etc.—and have your child place the cards on her desk to use as a reference. You may need to get permission from the teacher to allow your child to use these cards.

- Writing with a talking pen. Talking pens are special pens that give auditory feedback when letters are formed incorrectly. There are several versions available, including the Smart Talking Pen. You can go to www.nextag.com or ask about this product in office or school supply stores. Additionally, there is the Readingpen, which scans a word from any printed text, displays the word in larger print, reads the word aloud, and defines the word. This is a useful tool for any person struggling with reading difficulties. To order the Readingpen, go to the company's website at www.readingpen.com.

APPENDIX C

Resources

Throughout this book, a large variety of topics—including illnesses, disabilities, and academic difficulties—was discussed. There are numerous books and websites that provide more information on many of the subjects mentioned in this book. Here are some of the many resources.

ATTENTION DEFICIT DISORDER (AD/HD)

Attention deficit disorders are more prevalent than ever before. The following resources are beneficial tools for educating yourself about AD/HD.

Books About AD/HD and Brain Functions

Unless noted otherwise, all books are available through www.amazon.com.

ADD: The 20-Hour Solution by Mark Steinberg, PhD, and Siegfried Othmer, PhD. This book explains the self-healing capacities of the human brain for those with ADD and how it can learn, or re-learn, the self-regulatory mechanisms that are basic to its normal design and function.

Attention Deficit Disorder: ADHD and ADD Syndromes by Dale R. Jordan. This book talks about ADHD and ADD, along with providing information and understanding of this syndrome and how parents can help their children.

Change Your Brain, Change Your Life: The Breakthrough Program for Conquering Anxiety, Depression, Obsessiveness, Anger, and Impulsiveness by Daniel G. Amen, MD. In this book, Dr. Amen provides an easy-to-understand explanation of the biological basis for many disorders, along with strategies for overcoming many different problems, including ADD.

Healing ADD: The Breakthrough Program That Allows You to See and Heal the 6 Types of ADD by Daniel G. Amen, MD. Using breakthrough diagnostic techniques, Dr. Amen has discovered that there are six distinct types of ADD, each requiring a different treatment. He discusses his findings in this fascinating book.

Helping Your ADD Child: Hundreds of Practical Solutions for Parents and Teachers of ADD Children and Teens (With or Without Hyperactivity) by John F. Taylor, PhD. This book includes many solutions for parents and teachers of ADD children and teens.

Making a Good Brain Great by Daniel G. Amen, MD. This very popular book focuses on the brain in broad-based terms, explaining what it is and how to use it. The book creates awareness of the brain functions and how they impact upon everything we do.

A Symphony in the Brain: The Evolution of the New Brain Wave Biofeedback by Jim Robbins. In this book, the author traces the story of the development of neurofeedback, from its discovery to its growing application. Case studies, scientific explanations, and dramatic personal accounts are also included in the text.

AD/HD Websites

The following websites are useful tools for learning more about AD/HD.

The Amen Clinics, Inc. (www.amenclinics.com)
Amen Clinics believe changing your brain will change your life. Amen Clinics aims to improve the lives of every family it serves through education and the latest advances in neuroimaging and treatment options. It uses a variety of the least toxic, most effective treatments and individualizes treatment plans for every patient.

Attention Deficit Disorder Association (ADDA) (www.add.org)
ADDA is an international non-profit organization and the world's leading adult ADHD organization. Its goal is to provide resources, information, and networking opportunities to aid adults with ADHD in leading better lives.

Children and Adults with Attention Deficit/Hyperactivity Disorder (CHADD) (www.chadd.org)
CHADD is a national, non-profit organization that works to provide advocacy, education, and support to individuals with AD/HD.

EEG Info (www.eeginfo.com)
This website provides information about neurofeedback and its role in treating AD/HD.

AUTISM SPECTRUM DISORDER (ASD)

The following resources are beneficial tools for educating yourself about autism spectrum disorder.

Books About Autism Spectrum Disorder

Unless noted otherwise, all books are available through www.amazon.com.

Asperger's Syndrome: A Guide for Parents and Professionals by Tony Attwood, PhD. In his book, Dr. Attwood assists parents and professionals with the identification, treatment, and care of both children and adults with Asperger's Syndrome.

Biological Treatments for Autism and PDD by Dr. William Shaw. This guide-book provides useful treatments for autism, including antifungal and antibacterial therapies, gluten and casein restriction, homeopathy, vitamin therapy, gamma globulin treatment, and more.

Changing the Course of Autism: A Scientific Approach for Parents and Physicians by Bryan Jepson, MD, with Jane Johnson. This book shows that autism can be treated by reducing the neurological inflammation that is part of the disease process, rather than simply masking the symptoms with drugs like *Ritalin* and *Prozac*. The book reviews the medical literature regarding the biological nature of autism, including the potential connection between vaccines and autism.

The Complete Guide to Asperger's Syndrome by Tony Attwood, PhD. This is the definitive handbook for anyone affected by Asperger's Syndrome. It brings together a wealth of information on all aspects of the syndrome for both children and adults.

Facing Autism: Giving Parents Reason for Hope and Guidance for Help by Lynn M. Hamilton. This book is a treasury of detailed, helpful information from the mother of an autistic son. Hamilton has carefully investigated all of the promising treatment approaches for autism and discusses her findings in this book.

Hope for the Autism Spectrum: A Mother and Son Journey of Insight and Biomedical Intervention by Sally Kirk. This positive, practical book tells the author's personal story of hope as she copes with her son's diagnosis. It provides a wealth of essential information about biomedical interventions on the autism spectrum for both parents of children.

Like Color to the Blind: Soul Searching and Soul Finding by Donna Williams. In this book, Williams teaches us what it is like to be autistic and what it is like to be human, building a bridge between "my" world and "the" world.

Nobody Nowhere: The Extraordinary Autobiography of an Autistic by Donna Williams. Williams' autobiography is an attempt to come to terms with her autism. She aims to take the reader into the mind of an autistic person, providing an insider's view of a condition few people understand.

A Positive Approach to Autism by Stella Waterhouse. In her book, Waterhouse explores the relationships between autism and hyperactivity, ADD, obsessive compulsive disorder (OCD), and Tourette's Syndrome. Waterhouse also considers the advantages and disadvantages of some of the current treatments for autism, including secretin, diet, tinted lenses, and Auditory Integration Training.

Reweaving the Autistic Tapestry: Autism, Asperger's Syndrome, and ADHD by Lisa Blakemore-Brown. This book looks at the link between ADHD and autism spectrum disorder, providing a deeper understanding of the complexity of human development. Additionally, it introduces intervention and treatment plans for children with complex symptoms.

Sensory Perceptual Issues in Autism and Asperger Syndrome: Different Sensory Experiences, Different Perceptual World by Olga Bogdashina. In this book, Bogdashina attempts to define the role of sensory perceptual problems in autism as identified by autistic individuals themselves. The book singles out possible patterns of sensory experiences and the cognitive differences caused by them.

Thinking in Pictures and Other Reports from My Life with Autism by Temple Grandin. In this book, Grandin provides a unique and fascinating view of what it is like to think, feel, and experience the world as both a scientist and an autistic person.

Unraveling the Mystery of Autism and Pervasive Developmental Disorder: A Mother's Story of Research and Recovery by Karyn Seroussi. This book is a fascinating account of a determined mother and her scientist husband's success in bringing their son out of autism. It covers a wide range of topics and includes gluten and casein-free recipes.

Autism Spectrum Disorder Websites

The following websites are useful tools for learning more about autism spectrum disorder.

Autism Collaboration (www.autism.org)
Autism Collaboration aims to offer the most valuable autism answer-search facility available.

Autism Research Institute (ARI) (www.autism.com)
ARI is a non-profit organization dedicated to researching the triggers of autism and methods of diagnosing and treating the disease and disseminating the results of the research to parents and professionals around the world.

Autism Society (www.autism-society.org)
The Autism Society exists to improve the lives of anyone who is affected by autism. To do this, the society works to increase public awareness about the daily issues people on the autism spectrum face. It advocates for appropriate services for individuals and provides up-to-date information about treatment, research, advocacy, and education of the disease.

The National Autistic Society (www.autism.org.uk)
Located in London, the National Autistic Society champions the rights and interests of all people with autism and their families, providing help, support, and useful services.

Talk About Curing Autism (TACA) (www.talkaboutcuringautism.org)
TACA's goal is to provide resources, information, and support to families affected by autism. Additionally, TACA aims to accelerate the time

between autism diagnosis and effective treatments. It strengthens the autism community by connecting families and professionals and allowing them to share stories and information with each other.

Tony Attwood (www.tonyattwood.com.au)
Tony Attwood's website features a message board, chat room, and links to various autism and Asperger's Syndrome resources.

IRLEN SYNDROME

The following resources are beneficial tools for educating yourself—and your children—about Irlen Syndrome.

Books About Irlen Syndrome

Unless noted otherwise, all books are available through www.amazon.com.

The Light Barrier: Understanding the Mystery of Irlen Syndrome and Light-Based Reading Difficulties by Rhonda Stone. This book tells the story of one family's journey to understanding a reading barrier that may affect millions of children and adults worldwide.

Reading By the Colors by Helen Irlen. My first book (originally published in 1991) introduced Irlen Syndrome, at that time known as Scotopic Sensitivity Syndrome. The book presents the basic foundation of Irlen Syndrome and how it affects reading. Additionally, the book includes samples of the distortions as seen by those with Irlen Syndrome when they try to read a printed page.

Undiagnosed Up Until Now by Rod Groenhuizen. For a majority of his life, Rod suffered—unknowingly—from Irlen Syndrome. This book is his autobiography and shares Rod's story of how he believes the multiple conditions resulting from his Irlen Syndrome impacted his life. (To order, go to http://www.freewebs.com/undiagnosed/index.htm.)

Books About Irlen Syndrome for Children

All books are available through the Irlen Institute store at www.irlen.com.

Bratty-Cat, Blinky-Roo, and Snooze-Bear by Susan R. Smith. This beautifully illustrated book creates a wonderful tool to enhance awareness, acceptance, and information regarding Irlen Syndrome. This book is great for reading to your child or to the children in your child's classroom.

Jamie Lee and the Magic Glasses by Jay Luthy. This children's book tells the real story of how Jamie Lee struggled with reading and how she found help. Her new Irlen Filters changed her life!

LEARNING DISABILITIES

The following resources are useful tools for educating yourself about learning disabilities.

Books About Learning Disabilities

Unless noted otherwise, all books are available through www.amazon.com.

LD From the Inside Out: A Survival Guide for Parents by Carolyn Lampman Brubaker. A down-to-earth, realistic view of what really matters to kids and motivates them to learn. The book is filled with instructional strategies, successful practices, and learning activities all aimed to increase student achievement and enhance performance. (To order, go to www.carolynlampman.com.)

Overcoming Dyslexia in Children, Adolescents, and Adults by Dale R. Jordan, PhD. In this book, Dr. Jordan talks about the nature of dyslexia and how to overcome visual and auditory dyslexia. Additionally, he provides suggestions on how to develop social skills and independence.

The Queen of Education: Rules for Making Schools Work by LouAnne Johnson. In her book, Johnson discusses original solutions to intractable educational problems, offering down-to-earth advice about fixing schools.

The Seven Secrets of Learning Revealed: What Your Teacher Never Taught You Because Your Teacher Never Knew by Dr. Laurence D. Martel. This book helps people reach a place in life where learning can be fun. It includes successful strategies to provide the most useful information on learning and intelligence.

Shoot for the Stars! A Practical Guide for Helping Your Child Achieve Success in School and the Workplace by France Morrow, PhD. This book shows parents how to find their child's hidden barriers with reading and learning, as well as information on how to remove these often-invisible barriers once they have been identified.

Teaching Outside the Box: How to Grab Your Students by Their Brains by LouAnne Johnson. Written to help teachers define their own teaching philosophies, Johnson's book helps teachers develop positive discipline policies and experience the joys of teaching.

Learning Disabilities Websites

The following websites are useful tools for gaining more information about learning disabilities.

GreatSchools (www.greatschools.net)
Great Schools' mission is to improve education for children by getting parents involved.

Individuals with Disabilities Education Act (IDEA) (http://idea.ed.gov)
The site focuses on IDEA, the law that ensures services to children with disabilities throughout the nation.

Response to Intervention: A Primer for Parents (www.nasponline.org/resources/handouts/revisedPDFs/rtiprimer.pdf)
Response to Intervention is a process designed to help schools focus on high-quality, instruction-based interventions and instruction while carefully monitoring student progress.

Wrightslaw (www.wrightslaw.com)
This legal site contains accurate, reliable information about parent rights, special education law, education law, and advocacy for children with disabilities.

READING PROBLEMS

The following resources are useful tools for people who suffer with reading problems.

Comprehension

If your child has trouble comprehending the material when reading, try the following strategies.

Audio Books

Audio books are a great tool for struggling readers who are better able to obtain information by hearing it, rather than reading and absorbing it. The following companies are all great sources of audio books.

Audible (www.audible.com)
Audible is a great source for a wide selection of audio books available for download. In addition to books, Audible offers magazines, radio shows, podcasts, comedy, and speeches for download as well.

AudibleKids (kids.audible.com)
AudibleKids is an interactive community of parents, kids, and educators that promotes storytelling through audiobooks. The organization offers books for download, which can then be shared with others.

Books Aloud, Inc. (www.booksaloud.org)
Books Aloud, Inc. is a non-profit organization dedicated to improving the quality of life for people who cannot benefit directly from reading off a printed page.

Bookshare (www.bookshare.org)
Bookshare's goal is to provide people with disabilities access to the world of print. To do this, they have an extremely large selection of books and periodicals that are converted to large-print format or audio files. Bookshare offers titles from a variety of genres and even offers books in Spanish.

Kurzweil Educational Systems, Inc. (www.kurzweiledu.com)
Kurzweil's technologies provide reading, writing, and study solutions to aid all students in overcoming learning challenges so they can succeed academically.

Recording for the Blind & Dyslexic, Incorporated (RFB&D) (www.rfbd.org/membership.htm)
RFB&D helps students who struggle to read due to learning disabilities. it offers nearly every standard schoolbook from the leading K-12 publishers.

Talking Book World (www.talkingbookworld.net)
Talking Book World offers audio books, both as rentals and purchases. They have over 75,000 audiobooks.

Large-Print Books

For some struggling readers, books that feature a larger print ease strain and make the task of reading easier. In addition to school districts, libraries, and bookstores, you can find large-print books at the following sources.

Amazon (www.amazon.com)
Amazon is an online retailer offering products from a variety of categories. Type "large print books" into the search box to see what is available.

Doubleday (www.doubledaylargeprint.com)
Doubleday is a publisher that offers a wide variety of large-print books. The website above will direct you to its large-print selections.

Large Print Books (www.largeprintbooks.com)
This website offers a very extensive selection of large-print books from a variety of genres.

APPENDIX D

Finding an Irlen Testing Center Near You

To find a trained and certified Irlen Diagnostician or Irlen Screener in your area, go to www.irlen.com and click on "Find an Irlen Testing Center." Here, you will find a list of certified specialists located in the United States, Canada, South and Central America, Asia, Europe, Africa, New Zealand, and Australia.

The Irlen Method consists of two testing sessions: a screening appointment conducted by both certified Irlen Screeners and Irlen Diagnosticians, and a testing appointment for Irlen Spectral Filters which is conducted only by an Irlen Diagnostician.

Keep in mind that colored tinted lenses provided by others are *not* the same as Irlen Spectral Filters. Only certified Irlen Diagnosticians are trained to determine the specific color frequencies to optimize performance from an almost limitless selection of filters.

The Difference Between an Irlen Screener and an Irlen Diagnostician

Irlen Screeners are certified to administer tests to determine your symptoms, provide the best colored overlay, and determine the amount of improvement in reading comfort, fluency, and comprehension. Irlen Screeners will also identify the other areas that can be improved with the Irlen Method. With thousands of certified Irlen Screeners worldwide, only a few are listed on the website. To locate a screener nearer to you, contact your nearest Irlen Diagnostician.

Irlen Diagnosticians are certified to administer both the initial screening and subsequent testing sessions for Irlen Spectral Filters. The testing for Irlen Syndrome will be the same as administered by the Screener; but, in addition, other areas that affect attention, concentration, and performance are identified and a recommendation is made. Only Irlen Diagnosticians are certified to test and determine the color of customized Irlen Spectral Filters—worn as glasses or contact lenses—and conduct yearly rechecks.

References

CHAPTER 1

1. A synthesis of information from: Barnhart, Robert K. *American Heritage Dictionary of Science*, 1986.

2. Ornstein, Robert and Thompson, Richard F. *The Amazing Brain*. 1984.

3. Kolb, Bryan, and Whishaw, Ian Q. *An Introduction to Brain and Behavior*. 2004.

4. Krouse, S.L. and Irvine, J.H. "Perceptual Dyslexia: Its Effect on the Military Cadre and Benefits of Treatment." Presented at 45th Annual Conference of the International Military Testing Association, Pensacola, FL, 2003.

CHAPTER 2

1. Whiting, P.R.; Robinson, G.L.W., and Parrott, C.F. "Irlen Coloured Filters for Reading: A Six Year Follow-up." *Australian Journal of Remedial Education*. Vol. 26, No. 3. 1994, 13–19.

2. Alabama State Department of Education. www.alsde.edu/html/home.asp.

CHAPTER 3

1. U.S. Department of Education. www.ed.gov/index.jhtml.

CHAPTER 6

1. Mills, Evan. *Trends in Recommended Lighting Levels: An International Comparison*. www.iaeel.org/IAEEL/Archive/ Right_Light_Proceedings/Proceedings_ body/BOK2/200/2225.PDF.

2. Boyce, Peter. *Human Factors in Lighting: Second Edition*. London: Taylor and Francis, 2003.

3. International Energy Agency. *Light's Labour's Lost: Policies for Energy-Efficient Lighting*. OCED, 2006.

CHAPTER 7

1. Yellen, Dr. Andrew. "Irlen Syndrome and the Yellen-Schweller Effect." http://ezine articles.com/?Irlen-Syndrome-and-the-Yellen-Schweller-Effect&id=2102285.

2. Amen, Dr. Daniel G. "Brain in the News Newsletter." Amen Clinics, Inc., 2004.

3. Amen, Dr. Daniel G. "Letter: To Whom It May Concern." 2006.

CHAPTER 10

1. Kranowitz, Carol Stock and Silver, Larry B. *The Out-of-Sync Child: Recognizing and Coping With Sensory Integration Dysfunction*. Perigree Books, 1998.

2. Cantello, J. and Walker, N. *The Sensory Experiences of Individuals With Autism Based on First Hand Accounts*. Toronto, Canada: The Geneva Centre, 1994.

CHAPTER 12

1. Mayo Clinic. "Agoraphbia." www.mayoclinic.com/health/agoraphobia/DS00894.

About the Author

Helen Irlen, MA, BCPC, LMFT, a graduate of Cornell University, is a credentialed school psychologist, licensed therapist, adult learning disability specialist, and an expert in the area of perceptual processing disorders. While working with adults with learning disabilities, Irlen made a startling discovery that resulted in a marked improvement in her students' reading skills. Today, there are over 135 affiliated Irlen Testing Centers worldwide that use the Irlen Method to overcome a wide range of problems that can result from perceptual processing difficulties.

Index

60 Minutes
  Australian version, 23
  United States version, 23
  See also Irlen Method, discovery
    of, going public.

AD/HD
  differentiating between Irlen
    Syndrome and, 122–124
  difficulties diagnosing, 118–119
  Irlen Syndrome and, 117–127
  meaning of, 118
  medicating, 119–122
  misdiagnosing Irlen Syndrome as,
    120–121
  Thomas Edison and, 123
Agoraphobia, 169. *See also*
  Psychological disorders,
  misdiagnosing people with.
Amen Clinics, use of SPECT scan to
  study light sensitivity and Irlen
  Syndrome, 100–101
Anxiety, 171. *See also* Psychological
  disorders, misdiagnosing people
  with.
Attention deficit disorder. *See*
  AD/HD.

Attention deficit hyperactivity
  disorder. *See* AD/HD.
Autism
  common areas of difficulty with,
    133–136
  Irlen Method and, 139–140
  Irlen Syndrome and, 129–143
  making the connection to Irlen
    Syndrome, 130–131
  physical symptoms of, 137
  prescreening to see if Irlen
    Method can help, 139
  problem with treating, 137–138
  visual overload and, 132
  ways Irlen Filters can help, 141
Autism Society of America, 129
Autism spectrum disorder (ASD). *See*
  Autism.

Book markers, using, 67. *See also*
  Irlen Filters, strategies to use
  instead of.
Bookstand, using, 67. *See also* Irlen
  Filters, strategies to use instead of.
Brain function with light sensitivity, 96
Brain injury. *See* Head injury.
Brain surgery, Irlen-like symptoms
  and, 164–165

Bright lights, avoiding, 66. *See also*
    Irlen Filters, strategies to use
    instead of.
Brimmed hat, wearing, 67. *See also*
    Irlen Filters, strategies to use
    instead of.

California State University, 13, 62
Center for Advanced Medical
    Technologies, 100
Cerebral palsy (CP), 149. *See also*
    Irlen-like symptoms, medical
    conditions that lead to.
Chronic fatigue syndrome (CFS),
    149–150. *See also* Irlen-like
    symptoms, medical conditions
    that lead to.
Colored glasses. *See* Irlen Filters,
    colored glasses and.
Colored overlay. *See* Overlay,
    colored.
Colored paper. *See* Paper, colored.
Colors, as a trigger for headaches,
    110. *See also* Headaches,
    activities that cause.
Compact fluorescent lighting (CFL)
    bulbs. *See* Fluorescent lighting.
Computer work, as a trigger for
    headaches, 108–109. *See also*
    Headaches, activities that
    cause.
Conduct disorder, 169. *See also*
    Psychological disorders,
    misdiagnosing people with.
Contrast sensitivity, 153. *See also*
    Irlen-like symptoms, visual
    conditions that lead to.
Copying, as a trigger for headaches,
    109. *See also* Headaches,
    activities that cause.
Cornell University, 13

Depression, 169–171. *See also*
    Psychological disorders,
    misdiagnosing people with.
Depth perception
    Irlen Syndrome and, 85–89
    recognizing issues related to, 87
DESAR. *See* Visual Evoked Response
    (VER).
Discrepancy model of testing, 30
    issues not detected by, 32
    See also Learning disabilities,
    testing for.
Dominant eye theory, 19
Driving, as a trigger for headaches,
    109. *See also* Headaches,
    activities that cause.
Dyslexia, 75

Edison, Thomas, 123
Environment, Irlen Syndrome and,
    83–85
Environmental toxicity, 150. *See also*
    Irlen-like symptoms, medical
    conditions that lead to.
Epilepsy, light-sensitive. *See* Light-
    sensitive epilepsy.
Eye, parts of, 10
Eye/brain connection, 10

Fatigue, light sensitivity and, 96–97.
    See also Irlen Syndrome, light
    sensitivity and.
Fibromyalgia, 150–151. *See also* Irlen-
    like symptoms, medical
    conditions that lead to.
Florida Board of Optometry, 34
Fluorescent lighting, 93–96
Forty-Fifth Annual Conference of the
    International Military Testing
    Association, 10
Frostig, Marianne, 18

Frostig exercises, 18. *See also* Irlen Method, discovery of.

General Hospital, 23. *See also* Irlen Method, discovery of, going public.
Geneva Centre for Autism, 132
Glare, 153. *See also* Irlen-like symptoms, visual conditions that lead to.

Head injury, symptoms of, 159
  Irlen Filters and, 163–164
  making the connection to Irlen Syndrome, 161–164
Headaches
  activities that cause, 108–110
  determining if Irlen Method can help, 112–113
  indicators that someone is suffering from, 107–108
  Irlen Syndrome and, 103–115
  living with, 111–114
  medication for, 114
  migraines, 110–111
  misdiagnosing the cause of, 104–105
  mistreatment for, 105–106
  research on, 115
  triggers for, 106–107
Hemingway, Margaux, 23

Incandescent light bulbs, ban on, 93–96
  implication of, on people with light sensitivity, 96
Institute for the Visually Impaired, 154–155
Irlen, Helen
  work as a school psychologist, 9, 11–13
  work as the coordinator of California State University research component, 13–22

Irlen Diagnostician, 60–62
Irlen Filters, 62–66
  annual checks, 63–66
  autism and, 141
  causes of ineffectiveness, 64–66
  colored glasses and, 63, 154
  creating, 62–63
  head injuries and, 163–164
  improving light sensitivity, 97–98
  introduction of, 21–22
  strategies to use instead of, 66–68
Irlen Method
  autism and, 139–140
  challenges against, 26–27
  determining if headaches can be reduced with, 112–113
  difficulties with educational system, 31–34
  improving light sensitivity, 97–98
Irlen Method, discovery of
  bringing in experts, 16–17
  creating distortions for a control group, 17
  dominant eye theory, 19
  Frostig exercises, 18–19
  going public, 23–24
  independent research, 24
  initial reactions, 20–21
  initial research, 13–16
  introduction of colored glasses, 21–22. *See also* Irlen Filters, introduction of.
  screening children, 22
Irlen Screener, 60–62
  certification process to become, 60
Irlen screening, 58–62
  parts of, 58
  self-screening, 61
Irlen Spectral Filters. *See* Irlen Filters.

Irlen Syndrome
  acquired symptoms. *See* Irlen-like
    symptoms.
  AD/HD and, 117–127
  areas besides reading affected by, 82
  autism and, 129–143
  consistency of behaviors, 49
  definition of, 6–7
  depth perception and, 85–89
  environmental factors and, 83–85
  initial research on. *See* Irlen
    Method, discovery of, initial
    research.
  learning disabilities and, 27–31
  light sensitivity and, 91–102. *See
    also* Light sensitivity.
  psychological disorders and, 165–
    171. *See also* Psychological
    disorders.
  signs of, 48
  strategies and, 49–50
  studies on light sensitivity and,
    99–101
  timing of behaviors, 50–52
Irlen testing. *See* Irlen screening.
Irlen-like symptoms
  as a result of a head injury or
    psychological problem, 159–172
  as a result of a medical or visual
    condition, 145–157
  brain surgery and, 164–165
  environmental triggers of, 147
  medical conditions that lead to,
    147–152
  visual conditions that lead to,
    152–156
Irvine, James H., 10

Krouse, Susann, 10

Lasik eye surgery, 156. *See also* Irlen-

like symptoms, visual conditions
  that lead to.
Learning disabilities
  characteristics of, 28
  Irlen Syndrome and, 27–31
  lingo of, 35
  statistics about, 35–36
  testing for, 29–31
  See also Irlen Syndrome, learning
    disabilities and; Robert Robinson
    versus the Mobile County Board
    of School Commissioners.
Legally blind, 153–154. *See also* Irlen-
  like symptoms, visual conditions
  that lead to.
Light sensitivity
  acquired versus inherited, 92–93
  brain function and, 96
  fatigue and, 96–97
  Irlen Filters and, 93, 97–98
  Irlen Method and, 97–98
  Irlen Syndrome and, 91–102
  Irlen-like symptoms and, 153. *See
    also* Irlen-like symptoms, visual
    conditions that lead to.
  signs of, 95
  stress and, 97
  studies on Irlen Syndrome and,
    99–101
Light-sensitive epilepsy, 151. *See also*
  Irlen-like symptoms, medical
  conditions that lead to.
Low vision, 154–155. *See also* Irlen-
  like symptoms, visual conditions
  that lead to.

Macular degeneration, 155. *See also*
  Irlen-like symptoms, visual
  conditions that lead to.
Magnifying bar, using, 67. *See also*

Irlen Filters, strategies to use
  instead of.
Math, as a trigger for headaches, 109.
  See also Headaches, activities
  that cause.
MEG brain scan, 100. *See also* Irlen
  Syndrome, studies on light
  sensitivity and.
Migraines. *See* Headaches, migraines.
Movies, as a trigger for headaches,
  109. *See also* Headaches,
  activities that cause.

National Geographic, 23. *See also* Irlen
  Method, discovery of, going
  public.
National Headache Foundation, 104

Overlay, colored, 19–20, 62
  Irlen screenings and, 59

Panic attacks, 171. *See also*
  Psychological disorders,
  misdiagnosing people with.
Paper, colored
  using for assignments, 66
  using for tests and handouts, 66
  See also Irlen Filters, strategies to
  use instead of.
Parental rights, students' education
  and, 42–44
Patterns, as a trigger for headaches,
  110. *See also* Headaches, activities
  that cause.
Perceptual Dyslexia. *See* Irlen
  Syndrome.
Photophobia. *See* Light sensitivity.
Psychological disorders
  Irlen Syndrome and, 165–171
  misdiagnosing people with,
  166–169

Reading
  brain studies on, 78–79
  dyslexia, 75
  misconceptions about, 76
  schools and, 71–74
  struggles with, 69–71, 73–74
  ways parents can help kids'
  abilities, 75–78
Robert Robinson versus the Mobile
  County Board of School
  Commissioners, 34–35

Sally Jesse Raphael Show, 23. *See also*
  Irlen Method, discovery of,
  going public.
Schweller, Thomas, 97
  study on light sensitivity and Irlen
  Syndrome, 99–100
Scotopic Sensitivity Syndrome. *See*
  Irlen Syndrome.
Sensory Experiences of Individuals
  with Autism Based on First
  Hand Accounts, The, 132
Skip reading, 50. *See also* Strategies,
  Irlen Syndrome and.
SPECT (single photon emission
  computed tomography) scan,
  100–101. *See also* Irlen Syndrome,
  studies on light sensitivity and.
Standard answer test sheets,
  avoiding, 67–68. *See also*
  Irlen Filters, strategies to
  use instead of.
Steiner, Fritz, 154–155
Strategies
  determining usage of, 51
  Irlen Syndrome and, 49–50
Stress, light sensitivity and, 97. *See*
  also Irlen Syndrome, light
  sensitivity and.
Television, as a trigger for headaches,

109. *See also* Headaches, activities that cause.

Tourette's symdrome (TS), 151–152. *See also* Irlen-like symptoms, medical conditions that lead to.

University of Birmingham, 115. *See also* Headaches, research on.
University of California, San Diego, 99
University of Texas Medical School at Houston, 115. *See also* Headaches, research on.
University of Utah's School of Medicine, 100

Visual Evoked Responses (VER), 99.

See also Light sensitivity, studies on Irlen Syndrome and.
Visual overload, 132

Walking on Air (Roberts), 23. *See also* Irlen Method, discovery of, going public.
Wild About a Texan (Hudson), 23. *See also* Irlen Method, discovery of, going public.
Writing, as a trigger for headaches, 110. *See also* Headaches, activities that cause.

Yellen, Andrew, 97
study on light sensitivity and Irlen Syndrome, 99–100

DOES YOUR BABY HAVE AUTISM?
Detecting the Earliest Signs of Autism

Osnat Teitelbaum and Philip Teitelbaum, PhD

For many years, the diagnosis of autism has centered on a child's social interaction—from poor eye contact to lack of language skills. Although the autism community agrees that early intervention is key to effective treatment, the telltale signs of this disorder usually don't reveal themselves until the age of two or three. But what if it were possible to detect the potential for autism within the first year of life?

Osnat and Philip Teitelbaum have worked for nearly two decades to establish ways of detecting signs of potential autism or Asperger's syndrome by examining early motor development. This book first provides general information about the history of autism and The Ladder of Motor Development. Each of four chapters then examines one motor milestone—righting, sitting, crawling, or walking—contrasting typical and atypical development so that it's easy to recognize unusual patterns of movement.

$17.95 • 176 pages • 7.5 x 9-inch quality paperback • ISBN 978-0-7570-0240-3

CREATIVE THERAPY FOR CHILDREN WITH AUTISM, ADD, AND ASPERGER'S
Using Artistic Creativity to Reach, Teach, and Touch Our Children

Janet Tubbs

Thirty years ago, Janet Tubbs began using art, music, and movement to reach children with low self-esteem and behavioral problems. Believing that unconventional children required unconventional therapies, she then applied her program to children with autism, ADD/ADHD, and Asperger's syndrome. Her innovative methods not only worked, but actually defied the experts. In this book, Janet Tubbs has put together a powerful tool to help parents, therapists, and teachers work with their children.

Part One of *Creative Therapy* begins with the author's approach to balancing a child's body, mind, and spirit through proven techniques. Part Two provides a wide variety of exercises and activities designed to reduce hyperactivity, increase focus, decrease anger, develop fine motor skills, or improve social and verbal skills while helping children relate to their environment without fear or discomfort.

$18.95 • 336 pages • 7.5 x 9-inch quality paperback • ISBN 978-0-7570-0300-4

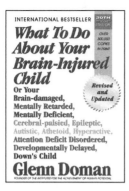

WHAT TO DO ABOUT YOUR BRAIN-INJURED CHILD

Glenn Doman

In this updated classic, Glenn Doman—founder of The Institutes for the Achievement of Human Potential and pioneer in the treatment of brain-injured children—brings real hope to thousands of children who have been sentenced to a life of institutional confinement.

In *What To Do About Your Brain-Injured Child,* Doman recounts the story of The Institutes' tireless effort to refine treatment of the brain-injured. He shares the staff's lifesaving techniques and the tools used to measure—and ultimately improve—visual, auditory, tactile, mobile, and manual development. Doman explains the unique methods of treatment that are constantly being improved and expanded, and then describes the program with which parents can treat their own children at home in a familiar and loving environment. Included throughout are case histories, drawings, and helpful charts and diagrams.

$18.95 • 336 pages • 6 x 9-inch quality paperback • ISBN 978-0-7570-0186-4

HOW TO MAXIMIZE YOUR CHILD'S LEARNING ABILITY

A Complete Guide to Choosing and Using the Best Computer Games, Activities, Learning Aids, Toys, and Tactics for Your Child

Lauren Bradway, PhD, and Barbara Albers Hill

Over twenty years ago, Dr. Lauren Bradway discovered that all children have specific learning styles—that is, they use one of three distinct ways to grasp and remember information. Some learn best through visual stimulation; others, through sound and language; and still others, through touch. In *How to Maximize Your Child's Learning Ability,* Dr. Bradway first shows you how to determine your child's inherent style. She then aids you in carefully selecting the toys, activities, and educational strategies that will help reinforce the talents and traits your child was born with, and encourage those skills that come less easily.

This book clearly explains the basic concepts behind Dr. Bradway's techniques, and offers practical guidance for supercharging your child's learning skills. Here are all the tools you need to start your child on the road to a successful future.

$14.95 • 288 pages • 6 x 9-inch quality paperback • ISBN 978-0-7570-0096-6